LifePrints

ESL FOR ADULTS

TEACHER'S EDITION

MaryAnn Cunningham Florez

New Readers Press

LifePrints: ESL for Adults Literacy Teacher's Edition
ISBN 1-56420-237-2
Copyright © 2002, 1995 New Readers Press
New Readers Press
Division of ProLiteracy Worldwide
1320 Jamesville Avenue, Syracuse, New York 13210
www.newreaderspress.com

Printed in the United States of America
9 8 7 6 5 4 3

All proceeds from the sale of New Readers Press materials support literacy programs in the United States and worldwide.

Acquisitions Editor: Paula L. Schlusberg
Content Editor: Judi Lauber
Production Manager: Heather Witt
Designer: Fran Forstadt, Shelagh Clancy, Kimbrly Koennecke
Cover Illustration: James P. Wallace
Production Specialist: Debbie Christiansen

Series Development: Robert Ventre, Inc.
                                Course Crafters, Inc.

Table of Contents

Introduction:
Using *LifePrints*

Welcome to *LifePrints*. This introduction to the Teacher's Edition will help you understand the rationale behind the program and the relationship among its various components. It will also explain the methodology inherent in the units of this Teacher's Edition (TE) and give you a step-by-step guide to conducting the suggested exercises and activities.

There are nine major sections in this introduction:

The core of the introduction is section VI, which describes the activities and exercise types for developing oral/aural language and reading and writing at this level.

I

Philosophy/Principles of the Program

LifePrints begins with the premise that adult language learners bring diverse life experiences that are rich sources of sharing in the ESL class. These experiences, together with the learners' current needs and desires, form the basis for learning the new language. By tapping into familiar roles and experiences, *LifePrints* allows such learners to see their past experiences as valuable in their new environment and helps them sustain their dignity during a time of transition.

LifePrints also assumes that adults enter the ESL classroom with a life-centered or task-centered orientation to learning. Adults perform many different roles in their daily lives. They are worker, spouse, parent, friend, citizen, and more. These roles often become sources of their self-identity. The role of student may be new and frightening to many adult ESL learners. They do

not necessarily want to learn *about* the English language; they want to learn to use English in performing their various adult roles. For them, English is not an end in itself; it is a tool with which to do something else. Adult ESL students are fully functional, at least orally, in their native language. *LifePrints* gives them the ability to start transferring to a new language and a new culture what they have done and can do as adults.

The organizing principle of *LifePrints* is not language; it is context. Language learning is contextualized in the everyday life experiences of immigrants, their neighbors, their co-workers. The lives of the characters in the book are entry points into the lives of the individual adult learners, and the lessons immerse the learners in situations where they can hear, see, and practice language that is relevant to contexts in their own lives. The linguistic and cultural skills presented in the pages of *LifePrints* are transferable to real contexts in the lives of adult ESL students.

Another principle of this series is authenticity. What would a native speaker hear, say, read, or write in a given context? What communicative role do English-language speakers play in a given situation? Are they primarily listeners, as when a doctor is giving them medical advice? Or are they speakers, as when giving someone directions to the library? Are they readers, as when looking up a telephone number? Or are they writers, as when completing a work log at the end of their shift? Or do they combine skills, like listening and writing when taking a telephone message, or reading and writing when completing a form? Learners are asked to practice only those linguistic skills that are authentic to the contexts or roles in which they will find themselves using English.

II

Principles of Second Language Acquisition

The acquisition of a second language is a complex process, representing a delicate balance between the learner and the learning situation. There is no single way in which all learners acquire another language. Many factors pertaining to each learner come into play, including age, preferred learning style, previous education, first language and its similarity to English, and motivation. The teacher has little control over these factors. What the teacher can do, however, is shape and reshape the language learning environment so that all learners have the greatest opportunity to acquire the English language skills they need to function as adults.

Throughout this introduction, we use the terms *acquisition* and *learning* interchangeably, irrespective of the cognitive processes involved. Some researchers and teachers contrast these two terms, assuming that they represent two different psychological processes. They apply *acquisition* to "picking up a language through exposure, using subconscious processes" and *learning* to "the conscious study of a second language." Other researchers and teachers argue that a sharp distinction between *acquisition* and *learning* is theoretical, not real. In both the acquisition and learning modes, basic principles underlie curriculum development.

These are some of the principles that guided the development of *LifePrints:*

- **The goal of language learning is communication in both oral and written form.** Learners should emerge from the language-learning classroom better able to understand and make themselves understood, as well as having greater facility in reading and writing English, than when they entered the classroom. Without being fluent in English, they can communicate on various levels, as described in the Student Performance Level chart (pages 22–23).

- **Communication is a process, not a sequence of memorized patterns or drill and practice exercises.** Function is more important than form. That is, what the learner *does* with language is more important than what he or she *knows about* language. Errors are therefore a necessary step in language acquisition. What is being communicated should be the focus, not the accuracy of what is said or correctness in the form of language. This is not to say that form—grammar, punctuation, and pronunciation, for example—is of no concern. Teachers need to focus on form, but at the right time in the learning process and in terms of furthering meaning. Too much attention to form too early will inhibit rather than encourage communication.

- **Language is most effectively learned in authentic contexts.** Contexts should reflect the world in which learners are expected to communicate in English, and as much as possible, they should come from the learners themselves. A corollary to this principle is that language is best presented not as isolated sentences or words but as meaningful discourse. The learning of grammar should also emerge from authentic contexts and should comprise a process by which learners discover patterns in language they already know and use.

- **Comprehension precedes production.** Learners need time to listen to language and to absorb what is happening in a variety of communicative situations. They need many and varied opportunities in which to be exposed to spoken and written English, using visual clues such as pictures, film and video, and realia (things from the real world that learners can see and touch).

- **Production of language, both oral and written, will most likely emerge in stages**. Beginning language learners will respond first nonverbally, then with single words, then with two- or three-word combinations, later with phrases and sentences, and finally by linking sentences together to form discourse. Particularly with literacy-level learners, this process may be noticeably recursive. There may often be periods when learners seem to move backward, using responses and behaviors characteristic of previous stages. Although learners should be encouraged to progress in their language learning, they should not be forced to produce language beyond their level of readiness or ability.

- **Key to student participation is a low anxiety level in the classroom**. For adults, language learning is by its nature an anxiety-laden pursuit. Literacy-level learners who have had limited exposure to classroom learning or negative educational experiences may find this anxiety compounded. The more the teacher and the textbook focus on "doing something with language"—for example, solving a problem, finding new information, describing a thing or situation, or buying a product—rather than on "learning language," the more likely learners will be to engage in the process of "acquiring" language. *LifePrints* will help the teacher establish a learning environment in the classroom where learners can actually function in English through task-oriented activities.

- **Linguistic skills should be as integrated as possible**. Adults interact with others and with their environment by using all their senses. By integrating listening, speaking, reading, and writing in meaningful, interesting, and interactive activities, *LifePrints* simulates the processes in which adults interact with their environment. This can be very important for literacy-level learners, who may come from cultures without a written tradition or may have spent much of their lives learning to compensate for their limited literacy. Integrating skills in the classroom as appropriate to the context or topic highlights and reinforces the interconnectedness of these skills in the real world. In the following pages we present some particularly effective listening, speaking, reading, and writing strategies. We suggest that these strategies be used together whenever it is feasible and authentic to do so.

III

Creating a Learner-Centered Environment

If language learning is to be successful, the learners' needs, not the grammar or functions of language, must form the core of the curriculum. Before discussing the creation of a learner-centered environment, we ought to look at who our learners are. Adult ESL learners are a diverse group ethnically, linguistically, and culturally. Some are immigrants, some are refugees, and some were even born in the United States. Some are newcomers, while others have lived and worked in this country for a long time. Some had strong academic preparation in their native countries but have weak oral skills; some have strong oral skills but weak or nonexistent literacy skills; and some have problems both with oral interaction and with reading and writing in English. Often these learners are grouped in the same classroom, so teachers will have to focus on the language needs of each type.

- Learners who have had academic preparation in their native countries must develop the practical oral language skills necessary to function in everyday life in their new cities or towns, to express their ideas in English, and to work in an English-speaking environment. These adults, who are likely to be newcomers to the United States, may even be comfortable with some reading and writing in English. Literacy in their native language is a part of their lifestyle, and they can use that literacy as a tool in learning a second language.

- Learners who have lived and worked in this country for a number of years have some oral English interaction skills, and they may have developed cultural coping strategies for living and working here. They may have limited formal education in their native countries or in the United States. Their literacy skills in any language may be low or nonexistent, and their academic and study skills may be lacking. Many of these learners come to the ESL classroom looking for programs that upgrade their oral English skills, as well as for literacy skills that prepare them to benefit from academic, vocational, or job-training opportunities.

- Learners who are new to the United States and who lack both oral and literacy skills needed to access information, express ideas, and solve communication problems in English are also likely to lack cultural coping strategies. They need strong developmental programs that help them acquire the language, literacy, and cultural skills necessary for learning and working in this country.

In addition to background, each adult comes with his or her preferred learning style. In general, *learning style* refers to one's preferred patterns of mental functioning. At least twenty different dimensions of learning style have been identified, far too many to detail here. Some people prefer to learn by watching, listening, and reflecting on their observations. Others are more comfortable learning by using abstract conceptualization, analyzing, and then acting on an intellectual understanding of the situation. Others learn best by doing and by active experimentation, while still others learn from feelings and specific interpersonal experiences. What this means for teachers is that a variety of strategies must be built into lessons so that all learners can draw on their preferred learning styles.

Teachers can use *LifePrints* to help learners with varying learning styles to observe, question, infer, and brainstorm—all activities that imaginative learners find useful. Full-page illustrations with prompt questions ("What's happening here? What do you think will happen next?") and semantic webbing are examples of activities that are effective with visual learners. Analytic learners can find patterns, organize, identify parts, and classify by means of activities such as using English to create charts and graphs. Commonsense learners can problem-solve, predict, experiment, and tinker with language. Dynamic learners can integrate, evaluate, explain, and reorganize the learning. In short, teachers using *LifePrints* can choose from a variety of activities that are consistent with students' learning styles and with their own. Research has shown that teachers tend to teach from and to their own learning style, so they should be aware not only of learners' needs but also of their own preferences and behaviors.

Creating a learner-centered environment is at the core of *LifePrints*. *Learner-centered* means that learners are in control of their own learning and direct what happens in the classroom. It also means that the curriculum is communicative-based rather than grammar-based and that language lessons center on relevant aspects of learners' lives. Finally, a learner-centered classroom calls for a collaborative effort between teacher and learners, with learners always playing an active role in the learning process. It is perhaps easier to describe than to define the learner-centered principles that guided the development of *LifePrints*.

- In an adult learner–centered class, learners and teacher become partners in a cooperative venture. The teacher creates the supportive environment in which learners can take initiative in choosing what they want to learn and how they want to learn it. This does not mean that the teacher has given up control of the classroom. The teacher must structure and order the learning process, guiding and giving feedback to learners in such a way that learners have the right amount of freedom. Too little freedom, as in a traditional teacher-centered curriculum, will stifle learners; too much freedom will make learners feel that the teacher has abandoned them.

- What happens in the language classroom should be a negotiated process between learners and teacher. The content and sequence of *LifePrints* lessons do not preclude the use of the program in a learner-centered curriculum. Indeed, the program is a starting point for classroom interaction and for student generation of adult learning materials. The language presented and practiced is based on issues, situations, and contexts that language-minority adults have expressed as crucial in their lives. Many of these same issues and situations will also be important in the lives of the learners in your class. The participatory process means that teachers must know their learners and ask them what they think and what they want to learn and do.

- Problem solving occupies a good portion of any adult's life, so it is not surprising that problem-solving activities are a necessary part of learner-centered curricula. Problem-solving exercises are prominent in *LifePrints*. In beginning units, learners are asked what they would say or do in a particular situation, or about their own experiences in similar circumstances. Later on, they are asked to present the pros and cons of a situation, to negotiate, or to persuade. Learners are also asked to generate problem-solving and simulation activities from their own lives. By presenting and solving problems in the classroom, learners become confident of their ability to use language to solve problems and to take action in the larger social sphere.

- The traditional roles of the teacher as planner of content, sole deliverer of instruction, controller of the classroom, and evaluator of achievement change dramatically in a learner-centered curriculum. When the atmosphere in the classroom is a collaborative one, the teacher becomes facilitator, moderator, group leader, coach, manager of processes and procedures, giver of feedback, and partner in learning. *LifePrints* lends itself to these roles, giving suggestions to the teacher for whole-class, small-group, paired, and one-to-one activities.

- In managing communicative situations in a learner-centered environment, teachers set the stage for learners to experiment with language, to negotiate meaning and make mistakes, and to monitor and evaluate their own language-learning progress. Language is essentially a social function acquired through interaction with others in one-to-one and group situations. Learners process meaningful discourse from others, and they produce language in response to other human beings. The teacher is responsible for establishing the supportive environment in which this can happen. This does not mean that the teacher never corrects errors; it means that the teacher knows when and how to deal with error correction and can help learners understand when errors will interfere with communication.

IV

The *LifePrints* Program

Encompassing four levels, *LifePrints* is designed to enable adult learners who have little or no oral and/or written competence in English to handle most everyday survival, social, and job-related situations independently, using oral and written English. The Literacy Level is designed for adults at Student Performance Level (SPL) 0; Level 1 is for those at SPLs 0–1; Level 2 for those at SPLs 2–4; and Level 3 for those at SPLs 5–6. A description of the SPLs appears on pages 22–23 of this Teacher's Edition.

The *LifePrints* program is composed of separate but linked components for each level. All four levels provide:

    (1) the Student Book (SB)
    (2) the Audiotape (▶️)
    (3) the Workbook (WB)
    (4) the Teacher's Edition (TE).

Levels 1, 2, and 3 also provide:

    (5) the Teacher's Resource File (TRF)
    (6) Assessment: Tests and Tools for Measuring Achievement.

At the Literacy Level, photocopy masters for TRF-style activities and for self-assessment are included in the Teacher's Edition.

The Basic English Skills Test (BEST) is an optional feature of the *LifePrints* program, providing a means for assessing placement and progress of adult ESL learners.

Student Book

The Literacy Student Book has six units, focusing on content and basic skills. In Levels 1, 2, and 3, there are 12 units in each Student Book. Ten (Units 1–5 and 7–11) focus on content, for example, housing, health, shopping, and employment; each concludes with a brief focus on selected grammar (structures) from the unit. The other two (Units 6 and 12) focus on key grammar (structures) that learners have used in the preceding units. A full Scope and Sequence for each Student Book, covering functions, structures, culture, and life tasks, is included in the Teacher's Edition for that book.

These are some of the features of all student books:

- Authentic language use at all levels.
- Adult contexts relevant to the lives of learners, their families, and friends.
- Visual stimuli for language learning, where appropriate, and a progression from visual to text-oriented material. While effective for all language learners, this progression taps into the natural learning strategies of low-literate individuals, who often use visual clues in place of literacy skills.
- An emphasis on paired and group work, because learners acquire language through interaction with others on meaningful tasks in meaningful contexts.
- Integration of listening, speaking, reading, and writing to reflect natural language use.
- Activities that help students transfer what they learn in the classroom to the world they live in.
- Grammar learning as a discovery process, with a focus on understanding the rules for language that students have already used and internalized. The discovery of rules is contextualized whenever possible.
- An integration of new cultural skills along with new linguistic skills. *LifePrints* recognizes that adults need to understand and acquire a layer of cultural behaviors along with language. The situations presented help learners to explore cross-cultural beliefs, attitudes, and values, and to compare and contrast expected behaviors in their native countries with expected behaviors in the United States.

Audiotapes

Because *LifePrints* learners are asked to engage in active listening, not to read conversations, there are no written dialogues in the student books. Instead, the audiotapes, an integral partner with the student books, offer real listening opportunities by providing all conversations on tape. In keeping with authentic language, they offer authentic listening practice, exposing learners to different voices and relevant listening situations in which learners will find themselves. Learners are given the opportunity to listen to a conversation several times, to ask questions about it, and to develop strategies for understanding what they hear. At the Literacy Level, audio activities also reinforce recognition and discrimination skills as learners develop phonemic awareness in their new language. Most important, learners at all levels are not forced to produce language they are not yet ready to produce.

Workbook

The *LifePrints* Workbook provides review and reinforcement activities coordinated to the language and content of each Student Book unit. The activities can be done individually or in pairs or small groups and are suitable for independent work outside of class. They provide targeted practice with selected structures, functions, and life tasks from the Student Book. Workbook activities provide additional opportunity for learners to practice reading and writing skills, but they can also be done or reviewed orally and provide additional stimuli for discussion, role play, and other oral practice.

Teacher's Edition

The layout of the *LifePrints* Teacher's Edition allows for a full view of each student page, along with the purpose of the lesson, materials needed, warm-up, presentation, and expansion activities. For each unit, the learning objectives are listed and categorized by linguistic functions, life tasks, structures, and culture. Key and related vocabulary are also provided for easy reference. Following is a description of the learning objectives sections in the TE, with suggestions on how to use them.

1. **Functions.** Functions focus on what people want to do with language or what they want to accomplish through oral communication. Functions can be categorized in different ways. The functions in *LifePrints* relate to personal matters, such as identifying oneself and one's family and expressing needs or emotions; interpersonal matters, such as expressing greetings and farewells, expressing likes/dislikes and approval/disapproval, persuading, and interrupting; and giving and seeking information by, for example, reporting, explaining, describing, asking, clarifying, and directing. An index of functions for this level of *LifePrints* appears on page 126.

2. **Life Tasks.** *Life tasks* refers to coping skills required to deal with aspects of daily life in U.S. society, such as shelter, employment, food, clothing, transportation, and health care. The life tasks included in *LifePrints* are listed in the Scope and Sequence. It should be noted that when put into the statement "The learner will be able to . . . ," these life tasks become functional life skills or competencies, correlating with adult competency-based curricula such as the California Adult Student Assessment System (CASAS).

3. **Key and Related Vocabulary.** For every subject or topic, some vocabulary is key, or content-obligatory; that is, without those words, one cannot discuss the subject. Other vocabulary is related, or content-compatible; these are words that modify, describe, or complement the key vocabulary. For each *LifePrints* unit, the most important key and related vocabulary is listed. At a minimum, learners should be able to understand these words in context. The subject matter and the proficiency level of the class usually determine whether the teacher should expect learners to use this vocabulary actively in conversation.

4. **Structures.** Although grammar is not isolated for practice in the core of each lesson, certain structures are primary and appear frequently in the lesson. In Levels 1, 2, and 3, many of these structures are highlighted at the end of each content unit and in Units 6 and 12, where learners are asked to discover patterns of grammar and then to practice the structures in new contexts. To help teachers give explanations where necessary, notes in the Teacher's Edition focus on the important features of a particular structure. The Scope and Sequence lists the primary structures for each unit, indicating whether they are introduced for the first time or are being recycled.

5. **Culture.** Items inherent in the subject matter of the unit that are cross-cultural (for example,

family, shopping, medical care, gender roles, and child-rearing) are noted in the Teacher's Edition. There is often a crossover between cultural points and life tasks. We suggest that, whenever possible, learners discuss cultural similarities and differences so they can reflect on ways of doing things in their native culture and of performing the same tasks in U.S. society, without making value judgments in either case.

Besides outlining the objectives for each lesson, the Teacher's Edition gives detailed suggestions for the teaching of each Student Book page. We use the word *suggestions* because the steps presented are meant as guidelines, not as absolutes. After considering the needs and learning styles of the learners in your class, as well as your own teaching style, you might blend them with the suggested steps for teaching the lesson. To feel comfortable with each student page, make your own lesson plan; include, along with the approximate timing, a "grab bag" of possible whole-class, small-group, paired, and one-to-one activities. Gather any needed materials well beforehand and, if you have time, practice-teach the page (without learners) to get a feel for the flow of the lesson, for monitoring your own speech, and for noting what you think might be difficult points for the learners. Suggested teaching steps include the following:

1. **Teacher Preparation and Materials.** Gathering materials is an important step, so the TE suggests the materials and any special preparation needed for the lesson. Most lessons require a cassette player for the listening activities, but other equipment and supplies may be needed as well. A language course that is contextualized in survival situations must rely on pictures and real objects to convey meaning. Building a picture file for the first time will take some work; however, after you have gone through the book with a class once or twice, the file will need only periodic updating. Highly visual magazines, mail-order and other catalogs, and newspaper advertisements and Sunday supplements are good sources of illustrations for survival situations. Pictures of houses; the inside of clinics/ hospitals and various workplaces; items in grocery stores, supermarkets, and department stores; and people interacting in both everyday and problem situations are examples of visuals for your file. Include pictures that can be used for sequencing and strip stories. In some cases you will want to cut and mount the picture before class; in others you will want to have learners look through a magazine or catalog to find

items as part of the class lesson. From time to time, the TE also suggests asking learners to provide pictures as out-of-class work.

For some units you will also need realia. An empty milk carton, an aspirin bottle, a soiled piece of clothing, a bus schedule, or a hammer and screwdriver can make the difference between learners really understanding and internalizing language and having only a vague idea of what a word or concept means. Particularly at the literacy, beginning, and intermediate levels of language learning, the gathering of materials is a crucial step in the teaching process.

2. **Warm-up.** The Teacher's Edition gives suggestions for getting started on a lesson and for eliciting concerns, information, and questions from the learners. Casual conversation with the whole group or a few learners, or small talk on a given topic, can be an icebreaker. Movement, chants, dances, and songs can both stimulate and relax learners so they are ready to attend to class business. The most important part of warm-ups for adult learners is tapping into their prior knowledge and experience and using their backgrounds to prepare for the lesson topic. Brainstorming activities that involve both learners and teacher in generating vocabulary, multiple associations, and illustrations on a specific topic can set the tone for the entire lesson. Warm-ups help learners organize information about a subject while lowering their anxiety level and getting them to use the English they have already acquired.

3. **Presentation.** This section is the heart of the Teacher's Edition in that it gives step-by-step suggestions for each page. It includes:

• Suggested language for asking questions and eliciting information. "Teacher talk" often gets in the way of the learners' understanding what they are supposed to do. In giving instructions, teachers sometimes use more complex grammatical structures than the learners can handle. Or they may talk too long, causing learners to lose track of what they are supposed to do. The suggested language in the Presentation section helps teachers avoid these pitfalls.

• Suggested activities or exercises. These activities—often introduced by "Have learners work in small groups to . . ." or "Using a semantic web, elicit from learners . . ." or the like—will help the flow of a lesson, though others can be substituted or added. You may need to adapt activities to the needs and proficiency level of the class, as well as to the characteristics of the learning site and your teaching style.

- Suggested teacher modeling and demonstration. Remember to model or give examples whenever possible. In activities such as completing interview grids, your asking a question first will make learners more comfortable in approaching their classmates.

4. **Expansion/Extension.** By giving suggestions for additional classroom practice, this section answers the common teacher lament "I've finished the Student Book, so what do I do now?" It functions as an idea bank both for whole-class exercises and for activities specifically geared to certain types of learners. The more advanced learners are challenged to be creative with the language they have acquired and to try out new language; slower learners are given opportunities for more work in problem areas. Some of the expansion exercises draw on the Teacher's Resource File, or TRF (see below). Others are variations of activities already done in class. Still others help move the language lesson from the classroom to the world outside, asking learners to do something new and immediately useful with the language they have acquired.

The Teacher's Edition also gives less experienced teachers insights into what might be going on when a learner or a class is faced with learning a certain function or structure. These insights come both from research into second language acquisition and from classroom practice. It helps teachers to know that when learners continually make mistakes with a certain structure, it is not because they haven't presented the structure correctly or given enough practice with it, but because, as research and experience have shown, the structure is acquired late and will remain a problem even for advanced learners. Similarly, it is helpful to know that, according to classroom experience, a particular exercise works better in small groups than with the whole class, or that learners must be at an intermediate language level before they can be expected to be aware of certain features of language, such as register. The *LifePrints* Teacher's Edition is designed to be used effectively by both experienced and less experienced teachers.

Teacher's Resource File

The Teacher's Resource File (TRF) extends the Student Book by giving teachers a wide variety of reproducible complementary activities. Only so much text can fit in a Student Book, so each TRF offers exercises, simulations, problem-solving activities, and games relevant to the themes of individual units, as well as generic games or game boards that can be used at any time. Because of the match between the Student Book and the TRF at each level, the Expansion/Extension sections in the Teacher's Edition often refer to specific TRF activities. Though an optional feature of *LifePrints,* the TRF is a resource that teachers can use over and over again, saving countless hours of planning and materials preparation. At the Literacy Level, reproducible TRF-style activities are provided in the Teacher's Edition.

LifePrints Assessment

The Assessment book for Levels 1, 2, and 3 of the *LifePrints* program provides achievement tests and informal assessment activities. The reproducible achievement tests, designed to be given after completing a level, include a listening skills test, a reading and writing skills test, and an oral skills test. Learners can be given one or all of these tests. Test activities are similar to the types of activities in the Student Book, so they accurately reflect how as well as what learners have studied. This familiarity is also designed to reduce test anxiety so learners can demonstrate with greater confidence what they have learned. There are two versions of each test, along with instructions for administering the tests, answer keys, and guidelines for interpreting results. In addition, there are detailed guidelines and suggestions for performance-based assessment activities and portfolio assessment. At the Literacy Level, the Teacher's Edition includes photocopy masters for self-assessment tools that learners and teachers can use to evaluate learning progress.

Basic English Skills Test

The Basic English Skills Test (BEST), another optional feature of *LifePrints,* assesses listening, speaking, reading, and writing in life-skills contexts. It contains two distinct parts: a one-to-one structured oral interview, which uses picture stimuli, and an individual or group-administered reading and writing section. BEST can be used both as a placement tool and as a progress test. Its scores are correlated with the Student Performance Levels (SPLs) of the Mainstream English Language Training (MELT) Project, as are scores on the California Adult Student Assessment System (CASAS). For a description of the SPLs, see pages 22–23.

V

Developing Literacy and Reading Skills at the Literacy Level

The Literacy Level of *LifePrints* is designed for learners at Student Performance Level 0. These learners function at a high level of oral proficiency in their native language and may be able to function at a minimal level of oral proficiency in English. However, in terms of their literacy skills, these learners may be nonliterate or preliterate. Or they may be unfamiliar with the Roman alphabet. *Nonliterate* refers to learners who come from a society or cultural tradition where written language either does not exist or is not used. *Preliterate* refers to learners who come from a literate society but who have not learned to read and write in that language. Other learners may be fully literate in the non-Roman writing system of their native language but have yet to master the Roman alphabet used in English. These distinctions can greatly affect the learning process. Teachers need to consider learners' experience with literacy in order to plan learning activities that are appropriate and effective for their specific learner group.

Two features of the Literacy Level warrant special mention. First, the Student Book is highly visual, relating pictures to meaning and stimulating learners to connect their current lives with their past experiences. Learners can focus on visual representations of thoughts or vocabulary, can relate what they are hearing on the tapes to clear pictures, and can begin to work with letters, numbers, and basic words in a variety of authentic contexts and formats.

Second, from the beginning, literacy is taught and practiced in meaningful contexts. The Student Book begins with an orientation to the language classroom to facilitate adjustment for learners with limited or no experience in educational settings. Learners are exposed to their names in an English-speaking environment, then their addresses and telephone numbers, then other vital information. In the early lessons, literacy is limited to important sight words—for example, personal names; addresses, including street names and numbers; telephone numbers; days of the week; and names of Student Book characters. Traditional reading and writing readiness skills, such as shapes discrimination or left-to-right/top-to-bottom progression, are not practiced specifically in the Student Book, but they

are included in the Workbook and as photocopy masters in the Teacher's Edition. Most units provide activities and suggestions to practice identifying letters, writing the alphabet, and working with sound/symbol correspondences, and teachers are encouraged to incorporate such practice as appropriate throughout the level. Activities in all components provide varied practice in basic reading and writing skills. Even at the literacy level, it is important to use literacy for authentic purposes immediately—for example, picking one's name from a pile of name tags and pinning it on so others can read it; writing names on a family tree diagram that can be used as a visual aid when learners talk about their families; or simply lining up under alphabetical headings as one often does in social service offices. All learners can participate in such authentic literacy activities. With literacy-level learners, the teacher will have to move more slowly, relying heavily on realia and other visual stimuli to elicit oral language, and working with learners individually and in small groups to develop literacy skills. Additional tips for working with literacy-level learners are found in section IX of this introduction (page 20).

Beginning second language learners often perceive their new language as undifferentiated noise. Literate learners take comfort in being able to see words written, or to write them down and then to look them up in a bilingual glossary or dictionary. Literacy-level learners cannot do this, so they must depend on short-term aural memory. Many will retain only a fraction of new material from one class to the next. Conventional ESL instruction, which delays reading instruction until such learners gain some oral proficiency, has frustrated many adult newcomers, who realize that literacy is an important part of their new society. These learners expect to be taught to read and write, as well as to understand and speak, from their earliest classes. The Literacy Level of *LifePrints* is designed to meet such expectations.

Two approaches to the teaching of reading are currently prominent: a skills-based model and a strategy-based model. In a skills-based model, the learner is asked to focus on pieces of language, for example, first sounds, then words, then phrases. Phonics-based instruction, such as decoding, is a skills-based model for teaching reading. In a strategy-based model, the focus is on both comprehension and production. *LifePrints* draws on a strategy-based model, with reading, writing, and oral language being mutually supportive components of a communications system that focuses on meaning. Literacy that focuses on meaning gives adult learners new ways to understand, control, and participate in new environments. It also enables them to tap into their background knowledge and to express something from their past.

While *LifePrints* adopts these meaning-based strategies, some phonics instruction can be of value. English does use an alphabet, which means there is a sound-symbol correspondence, and phonics may help learners visualize the written form of words they have already acquired orally. The important point to remember is that all skills must be a part of, not separate from, meaningful communication. The next section describes in more detail *LifePrints* activities that develop reading and writing, as well as listening and speaking, through a focus on meaning.

VI

Features of the Literacy Level Student Book Lessons

1. First and Last Pages

The first page of every lesson is a full-page visual that introduces a main theme. It also taps into previous knowledge and experience, and into the vocabulary learners might already possess. By pointing to objects in the picture or asking questions such as "What do you see?" "Where do you think they are?" and "Do you have (name of objects) in (name of learner's native country)?" the teacher elicits or provides vocabulary, gives learners a chance to answer and ask questions about a visual stimulus, and "hooks" learners into the lesson. At this point, the teacher will want to write the vocabulary on the board and/or prepare a set of word and picture flash cards that can be used throughout the lesson.

The last page of every lesson gives learners a chance to review and synthesize what they have learned in the lesson and to use their new reading and writing skills by doing something authentic with language: checking items on a grid, writing personal information, completing a form, and so on. It also gives learners a chance to review vocabulary, connect it with what they have learned, and extend it to new situations outside of class.

Between the first and last pages, a variety of language presentations and exercises introduce and give practice in listening, speaking, reading, and writing holistically, that is, as interacting parts of a complete system. There is no set pattern. Authentic language situations often call for one skill more than another. For instance, a visit to a doctor's office elicits listening and speaking practice primarily, while checking a bus schedule or peering at the small print on a bottle of cough medicine requires reading primarily. The flow of the Literacy Level follows the situation and the language needed to cope in that situation. Each lesson, however, focuses on the correspondence between oral language and written representation of meaning.

2. Activity and Exercise Types

The Student Book contains various exercise and activity types, including question-answer, matching, charts, identification, interview, fill-in, labeling, and word completion. Basic skills are developed through extensive opportunities for tracing and copying. Other activities or exercises are suggested in the Teacher's Edition for each page—for example, using graphic organizers such as semantic webs, doing a Total Physical Response (TPR) activity, using a substitution drill, playing games such as Concentration, and creating a Language Experience Approach story. The following are short step-by-step instructions for many of the exercises and activities that appear either in the Student Book or in the Teacher's Edition. Instructions that are self-evident, as for matching and question-answer activities, are of course not included.

Listening/Speaking Activities

Until recently, listening was considered the passive skill and speaking the active skill in aural/oral communication. We now see that good language learners are active participants in the listening process, not just passive recipients. Literacy-level listening activities, in which learners must respond with action or demonstrate comprehension, help learners start developing strategies for active listening. They are also effective lead-ins to the speaking activities.

- **Total Physical Response (TPR).** *TPR* refers to listening/action activities, which are excellent for a literacy-level class. The general objective of TPR is to teach the spoken language through the performance of actions in response to commands. Essential to TPR are concrete action verbs that can be used in the imperative form. However, the approach does not limit the teacher to simple physical commands, such as "Walk," "Jump," "Get up," and "Sit down." More complex commands can be used, for example, "Point to the teacher's desk," and "Find all the signs in the picture."

Steps for Using TPR

1. Say new vocabulary words or phrases in command form and model the meanings. (For example: "Touch your head." "Jump.") Learners respond by doing each action.

2. Command and model again. In a large class, first command and model with all the learners, then with a small group, then with an individual learner.

3. Command without modeling, and have a large group, a small group, or one learner respond by doing the action.

4. Recombine old and new commands with and without modeling. Learners respond by doing each action. If they show any confusion during this or the previous step, immediately return to modeling the actions for them.

Variations

Change the order of commands to increase interest, or change the kinds of groups being commanded (small group, large group, pairs, individual, etc.). Learners listen more carefully when they cannot anticipate what will be said or who is being addressed. If learners are comfortable, allow them to issue the commands or to be part of a whisper command chain, starting with you. As a challenge, you can turn TPR into a game of Simon Says.

- **Listen and Do.** Because listening is such a key skill at beginning levels, exercises that foster listening and then responding by doing something are important motivating activities. In general, it is a good idea to ask learners to listen to each activity prompt or short conversation on the audiotape at least three times.

Steps for Using "Listen and Do"

1. Play the taped activity or conversation and have learners listen. For conversations, have them look at pictures in the Student Book in order to understand the situation, identify the speakers, and gain overall meaning. At this point learners are not asked to take any action, only to listen and perhaps to look at a certain page in their book.

2. For conversations, ask learners *Yes/No* and *Wh-* questions about what they heard as a check on their literal comprehension, interpretation, and so on. Such questions as "What is Susan's last name?" "Where does Alex live?" and "When does Robert work?" will let you know if learners have the gist of

the conversation. Ask learners if they have any questions.

3. Tell learners that you will play the tape a second time. Ask them to listen for specific information that appears in their books, in either written or picture form (numbers, places, or people, for instance), or for words, numbers, or sounds used in an activity. Play the tape a second time and have learners do the activity called for in their book (or one that you create), perhaps circling, underlining, matching, checking, writing, or filling in.

4. Play the tape a third time, asking learners to check their answers. You should check for overall understanding of a conversation as well.

Variations

The second listening can be broken into two steps, the first time for homing in on the desired information and the second for doing the activity in the book. A fourth listening then becomes the answer/comprehension check. You can also play only snippets of a conversation or activity to help learners focus on meaning in more manageable bits of language.

While the audiotape provides extensive listening opportunities, you can expand them even further. Here are suggestions for sharpening listening skills with a focus on the Literacy Level Student Book pages:

- Have learners look at a page that has a story or several pictures. Compose and read a very basic description of one of the pictures (or read the caption underneath) and have learners choose from the set of pictures the one that is being described.

- Have learners focus on the picture on the first page of a unit. After you have done the activities suggested for that page, say the names of various items in the picture and have learners point to them.

- Say the names of various characters or objects in the Student Book and have learners find and point to them. Or compose simple descriptions of characters in the book and have learners find and point to them.

- Once learners know the words for places in a community, say the name of a local bank, drugstore, school, etc. (for example: National Bank or Foodway Supermarket) and have learners identify and/or write the general place word in the name *(bank, supermarket)*. Then say other names and have learners identify the type of place it is.

- Have learners draw a stick figure of a person and then add body parts as you say them. Use obvious, easily drawn parts like hand, foot, ear, nose, eye, and so on.

"Listen and do" exercises are limited only by your imagination. Just remember that, at this level, learners cannot handle a very complex activity or very much language at one time.

- **Chain Drills.** Chain drills are good icebreakers for learners at beginning levels, because they are a form of finite and controlled communication. They should not be used too often or too long because they can get very boring. They should be used with a meaningful communicative purpose. For example, one learner asks another, "Where are you from?" The second learner answers and then asks another learner the same question. This is a communicative activity the first few times, but if learners do the same drill ten times, or if forty learners make up the chain, the drill is no longer communicative; you should therefore keep chain drills short and mix them with other activities.

Steps for Using Chain Drills

1. Model the activity by asking a question or greeting a learner, saying, for example, "Where are you from?" The learner answers you ("I'm from Haiti"), then turns to another learner to ask the same question you asked.
2. In groups forming a circle or line, the first learner greets or asks a question of the second learner.
3. The second learner responds and asks the question of the third learner.
4. The third learner responds and continues the chain.

Variation

Learners form a circle. One learner addresses a question to the whole circle and then tosses a ball to an individual learner. The catcher answers the question, asks the whole circle the original question, and tosses the ball to another person. And the game continues.

- **Structured Interviews.** In a common Literacy Level activity, one learner asks another for information. Learners can record the information on a chart or grid by making a check mark, writing or circling *yes* or *no*, or writing a number or name. At first, little literacy is required, though learners have to understand how to read and use charts and interview grids, as in grasping the function of headings across the top and down the left side.

Steps for Using Structured Interviews

1. Have learners form pairs, or pair the learners yourself. The interview process works best if the partners do not know each other well.
2. One partner interviews the other.
3. The partners reverse roles. Both partners record the results of the interview.
4. The results of the interviews are shared, with either the whole class or with a group composed of three to six pairs. Each learner speaks for the person he or she interviewed.

Variations

Depending on his or her ability, one learner can interview from three to six classmates, not just a partner. Interviews are excellent activities for multilevel groups because learners can give longer or shorter answers according to their ability. Higher-level learners can even create their own interview questions. The Student Interview Chart (Handout 5 in the photocopy masters at the back of this Teacher's Edition) can be adapted for a wide variety of interview activities.

An extension of the interviewing activity has learners lining up for various reasons. For example, in Unit 2, learners can use an interview grid to ask classmates if they are married or single. After the interviews are completed, have all married learners form one line and all single learners form another line, counting the number in each. If an interviewer asks "What country do you come from?" have learners line up in alphabetical order by country.

- **Semantic Webbing.** Semantic webbing is a form of graphic organizing in which learners and teacher work together to make connections between ideas and the vocabulary inherent in those ideas. Besides being an excellent whole-class warm-up activity, semantic webbing builds vocabulary by asking learners for information and language they already possess, and it links that information and language with new vocabulary. Moreover, learners can use the webs throughout the unit for both oral and written work. For literacy-level learners, be sure to keep the webbing activities and connections between words clear and simple until learners are comfortable with the format. If possible, reinforce the meaning of words by drawing or taping pictures next to words on the web. An example of a semantic web appears below.

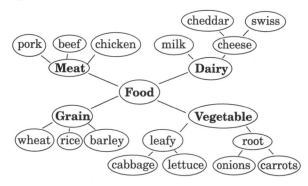

Steps for Using Semantic Webbing

1. In the center of the board, write a word referring to the topic of the unit. Be sure learners understand the word by asking them for an explanation, description, or examples.

2. Ask learners for related vocabulary, trying to elicit the unit's key words. Organize the words as much as possible into categories, as in the example above.

3. Have learners copy the web in their notebooks. Keep a copy for class use.

4. Refer to the web during the unit, adding vocabulary where appropriate.

Variations

Other graphic organizers can help learners store and categorize new information. For example, time lines allow learners to organize and sequence events chronologically. Flowcharts show progression, sequencing, and cause and effect.

- **Substitution Drills.** A major focus of the *LifePrints* Literacy Level is the acquisition of vocabulary. New vocabulary is always introduced and practiced in meaningful contexts. At the literacy level, substitution drills can help reinforce vocabulary recognition and add new words in similar semantic categories.

Steps for Using Substitution Drills

1. Tell learners you want them to replace a certain word in a sentence. Model by giving a sentence and saying the word you want learners to substitute. (For example: "Today I feel happy—angry.") The next sentence is "Today I feel angry," with another cue word coming after *angry*.

2. You can lead the drill and have learners do the substituting, or you can have a learner lead the drill. Try to elicit authentic, relevant substitutions whenever possible.

Variations

You can combine substitution drills with other drills, starting with a chain drill. To make a drill harder, give two or more slots (words) that need substitutions, or use visual cues (pictures, photos) and have learners supply the vocabulary. To make a drill more communicative, have learners add a sentence, such as "Today I feel happy. I got a letter from my best friend."

- **Paired Exercises.** Many exercises in *LifePrints* call for learners to work with a partner. The following technique, sometimes called "Think-Pair-Share," is a cooperative learning activity that allows learners to share information and ideas; it is also useful for tapping into prior knowledge and building vocabulary. It is an excellent way to deal with the first page of each unit or with other pages that contain large visuals.

Steps for Using Paired Exercises

1. With a visual stimulus (for example, a picture or realia), ask learners to think about vocabulary associated with the picture or item.

2. Learners think to themselves and, if they can, list the vocabulary.

3. Learners form pairs to compare and discuss their lists.

4. Learners share their vocabulary with the class while you list all the words on the board.

5. During the unit refer to these words. By the end of the unit, make sure that learners understand them in context.

- **Role Play.** In some instances the Literacy Level Teacher's Edition suggests role-play activities. These activities put learners in situations similar to ones they have already practiced through activities involving the characters in the Student Book. Typically, one learner takes a role in a given situation, and another learner (or the teacher) takes the other role in the conversation. Role plays at the literacy level might consist of one learner calling for an appointment with the doctor. Or one learner might pretend to be looking for a job and the other might offer advice.

Steps for Using Role Play

1. Tell learners to imagine themselves in a given situation. Be as explicit and descriptive as possible.

2. Ask learners to play specific roles in this situation, or ask a learner to play one role while you play the other. (You will want to

take part in role plays where you think the language would be too difficult for learners to produce or where you think they might feel uncomfortable.)

3. Ask learners to behave as if the situation were real and to have a conversation using language appropriate to their roles.

Variations

Effective role plays for adults involve problem solving. The problem should be relevant to the learners and to the topic they have been studying. Set the scene by telling a story or narrating a situation. For example: "Your ear hurts, and you have a sore throat. You call the doctor. What do you say to the receptionist?" Have individual learners, pairs, or small groups prepare and then present what they would say.

Reading/Writing Activities

After learners initially learn to read, they then read to learn or to do. Along the way they also learn to write, and the writing in turn helps them to read. As literate persons they will read for information, meaning, directions, or pleasure. Many learners at the literacy level will be just learning to read and write. The following activities will be helpful in that process.

- **Language Experience Approach (LEA) Stories.** In creating LEA stories, the learners' own words are used as the material for reading and then writing. LEA stories are good for practicing not only literacy skills but also aural/oral skills. The advantage of language experience stories is that they are learner-generated materials; as such, they hold the learners' interest and are never too difficult or too easy. Learners will provide only stories that are within their language capabilities. All learners can participate, adding what they can to the story. At the literacy level, they may produce only words and phrases to convey the story. The word *story* can mean a narrative, but also a description, instructions, explanations, and the like. There are many ways to do LEA stories. This is one of them:

Steps for Creating LEA Stories

1. Using the visuals in the Student Book or any other pictures that evoke a story or situation that learners may find of interest, go around the room, giving each learner the opportunity to contribute to the story. Stimulus questions, such as "What do you think is happening?" "What is that?" and "Who is doing (some action)?" are helpful if learners do not respond spontaneously.

2. On the board, write what the learners dictate. Do not correct at this point, as this would serve only to discourage and inhibit learners. The learners are expressing what they want to say in the way they know how to say it. However, it is acceptable for other learners to make corrections.

3. When the story is finished, read it aloud to the learners and have them repeat it.

4. Point out certain vocabulary for special practice and repetition.

5. Sometime later, edit the story for corrections and type it up to make a copy for each learner.

6. During a following class, distribute the story and review it in final form.

7. Have learners keep a folder of all their LEA stories so they can always have reading materials they can understand.

Variations

Variations include doing an individual language experience story with each learner. The stories can be based on a picture or on learners' experiences (vacations, celebrations, coming to the United States, etc.). Many activities can be created from the learner-generated stories. For example, sentence strips can be made and the order of the story rearranged. Sentences can be cut up and rearranged for practice with grammatical structures and word order. The vocabulary can be worked into new learner-written dialogues. And the stories can be made into cloze exercises.

- **Learner-Produced Picture Books: A Class Library Project.** It is very important for beginning ESL learners who are new readers to realize that they can write as well as read. One good technique is having learners produce books that then become part of the class library. Learners might produce books that go with the topics of the units (about, for example, "the neighborhood around our school" or "jobs in my native country").

Steps for Using Learner-Produced Books

1. Distribute or have learners bring in picture magazines such as *National Geographic* or *People,* as well as mail-order catalogs and the like, that can be cut up.

2. Each learner finds a picture of interest, clips it, and mounts it on a sheet of paper.

3. Ask learners to write something about the picture on another sheet of paper. They may write only one or two words, or they may ask you to write down what they say. More

advanced learners may write more detailed pieces.

4. Correct what the learners write to make it comprehensible; that is, do not correct every mistake, but enough so the message is clear.

5. Have learners produce clear, neat, corrected copies of what they wrote.

6. Repeat this activity throughout the course. Near the end, have learners assemble their pictures and written work into books for the class library.

Variations

Have learners develop a cultural resource library. Ask them to find pictures or bring in photographs from their native countries and then to write about those countries and about the visuals in particular. Developing books can also be a group project, with a learner at a higher level of language and literacy acting as the group leader.

- **Strip Stories.** Strip stories can be done in pairs or small groups. Learners each have one piece or strip of a story, a set of instructions, or a conversation, and together they must put the pieces in logical order. This exercise can be used with stories in the Student Book, with materials provided in the photocopy masters, or with learner-generated texts.

Steps for Using Strip Stories

1. Cut a reading passage, a conversation, or a set of instructions/directions into parts. Parts may consist of a word, a phrase, or a sentence.

2. Tell learners that they must reconstruct the whole by putting the parts in the right order.

3. Working in pairs or small groups, learners read their pieces to each other and reconstruct the story by numbering or rearranging the pieces.

4. Have learners read their reconstructed work to the class, and have the class judge whether or not the task has been successfully completed.

Variations

A complete story may be too challenging for literacy-level learners in the beginning stages. As an alternative, you can use the same concept to have learners use letters to make words like *hello* or *name,* or they can use words to construct simple sentences. As learners progress, you can ask them to reconstruct conversations or stories from the book.

This is by no means an exhaustive list of exercises and activities. You will find that, as you use them, some will be more comfortable for you and your learners than others. You will also find yourself inventing your own variations.

In conducting any of the exercises or activities listed above, remember that literacy-level learners need ongoing contextual support for the vocabulary and structures that they are learning. It is important to continually prompt their awareness that print conveys a meaning or corresponds to an action, item, or idea. Use gestures, facial expressions, pictures, and realia to make words and concepts concrete and to make connections between meaning and print obvious, comprehensible, and memorable.

Strike a balance between routine and variety in activities. Patterns and routines offer a sense of familiarity and security that can support literacy-level learners as they tackle new vocabulary or structures. Repetition is necessary and often is not as boring for the learners as it may appear to the teacher. Building redundancy into the lessons, such as asking learners to use numbers for counting in one unit, for reading prices in the next, and for telling time in the next, gives them the ongoing opportunities for practice that they need. However, it also asks them to look at words and numbers in different contexts, attaching new vocabulary and concepts to information that they are already in the process of mastering. While they may have limited skills, literacy-level learners still need activities that challenge them, speak to different learning styles, and keep them interested. In particular, to facilitate their own transfer of skills, learners need to see how oral and written language is used in authentic contexts within and outside of the classroom. The key for the teacher is in providing the preparation and support that will help them do this.

3. Structures

In *LifePrints,* grammar is a discovery process in which learners are exposed to and use structures in context in the thematic units. In working with beginning-level learners, the emphasis should be on communication over accuracy, on function over form. At the literacy level, learners use and practice language segments or "chunks" that exemplify common structures in English. The focus is on exposing learners to these structures and giving them constant opportunities to grow accustomed to using the structures within the normal communicative flow of English. At the same time, learners acquire words and phrases that they can immediately connect with and use in their lives outside the classroom. At later levels they can focus more explicitly on these structures and begin to develop accuracy.

4. Vocabulary

Vocabulary is traditionally a focus at the literacy level. However, remember that vocabulary is best taught in context, as part of communicative listening, speaking, reading, and writing activities. Isolated lists of vocabulary that learners memorize do not lead to meaningful use. New words and phrases become internalized to the point where learners will use them in new situations after multiple opportunities for use. Vocabulary-building and internalizing activities include flash cards, semantic webbing, matching words to pictures, labeling, TPR, and other exercises that require following directions. As learners progress through the unit, recycle vocabulary from previous lessons. If possible, keep on display word lists and semantic webs that learners have made, referring to and checking off vocabulary that learners seem to have mastered. This gives beginning learners a powerful tool for seeing how much they have learned. Prompt learners to use new vocabulary in LEA stories and to read those stories several times as you go through the units. There are many ways to exploit each activity to reinforce vocabulary.

5. Culture

Language and culture are integrally bound, so learning a new language means understanding a new culture. Culture is the institutions and shared behavior patterns of a society. But it is also the values, attitudes, and beliefs that underlie the institutions and behaviors. How we think about family is culture-bound. So is our attitude toward gender roles, competition, and medicine. From the beginning units, ask learners to reflect upon their experiences in the United States in terms of what things were like or how they did things in their native countries. The first unit, on the classroom, might be a good place to start. In several places, the Teacher's Edition suggests asking learners to compare their new classroom and the learning environments in their native countries. You as the teacher help learners understand cross-cultural situations. Start from learners' native cultures to help them explore their new one. You and other learners can learn much.

6. Pronunciation

There are no overt pronunciation exercises at the Literacy Level of *LifePrints*. Throughout the Student Book, however, there are a number of exercises that target recognition of sound-symbol correspondences. Teachers are encouraged to use these exercises or create similar ones to foster development of this skill. The addition of sound-discrimination listening activities or minimal-pair *(pat/bat)* speaking activities can also be beneficial to adults developing literacy because they practice hearing and producing the sounds of the language. In providing examples of natural speech, the audiotapes are good models. You may want to point out specific sounds, words, or intonation patterns and have learners practice them. In general, however, attention is better devoted to fostering communication.

VII

Testing and Assessment

Testing and assessment are core parts of teaching and provide valuable feedback to learners and teachers as well as program administrators and funders. At the literacy level, there is always a concern that learners might find the concept of testing unfamiliar and even intimidating. At this level, it is more important for learners to be able to perform, to demonstrate what they can do with language, and to be able to recognize and assess their own progress than to pass formal tests.

To familiarize learners with the process of self-assessment, three "Checking In" self-assessment sheets, one for every two units in the Student Book, are provided as photocopy masters in this Teacher's Edition so that you can help learners review and evaluate how they feel about what they have studied. These sheets list the principal concepts covered, with spaces for learners to record what they feel they know or do not know after completing the units. You can then review the sheets with learners, showing them how much they have learned and noting what still needs practice. Focus on what learners still want to accomplish so that, whenever possible, you can individualize instruction.

In addition to the self-assessment sheets, you may also want to create performance-based checklists or work with learners to create learner-generated learning logs that can record vocabulary, structures, and skills mastered in the course of a unit. Again, this puts the focus on learners demonstrating what they have accomplished and what they can do with language, rather than what they have learned about it.

VIII

Classroom Management

Adult ESL classes usually present a wide variety of factors that can affect class management. Most of you will have multilevel groups or classes. Despite the fact that literacy-level learners all share similar needs in development of reading and writing skills, there can be significant differences in their proficiency levels in other language skills, in educational and cultural backgrounds, and in motivation and goals. Some of you will also teach in open entry/open exit situations. Others will have impossibly large classes. *LifePrints* strongly emphasizes pair and small-group work as a means of meeting these challenges. While pairings and groupings will not solve all classroom management problems, they offer many advantages. When the class is actively engaged in pair or small-group work, everyone is communicating. For a learner who is uncomfortable speaking in front of the class, for instance, pair work offers an audience of one. Small-group work allows that same learner to contribute what he or she can, relying on others to both add and stimulate.

Pairings are of three types: random, voluntary, and assigned. It is a good idea to vary pairings so learners get to work with different members of the class. Random pairs are generally formed by asking two learners who are sitting next to each other to work together. Random pairs can work together for active listening practice, conversation, completing exercises, cooperative writing, and reviewing each other's work. When learners form voluntary pairs, they are likely to gravitate toward a classmate with whom they feel comfortable. Often this is someone who speaks their native language, so expect to hear some non-English conversation. You should use voluntary pairs when English must be produced, as in the preparation and presentation of dialogues, the creation and ordering of strip stories, and interviews outside of class that require interaction with native speakers. Assigned pairs are usually based on proficiency levels. If you pair learners with similar abilities, they can work together at the same pace or they can correct each other's exercises. At other times, assigning partners of different levels is helpful because the more advanced learners can quietly help the less advanced. Both learners benefit: the less advanced are generally not threatened, and the more advanced gain valuable practice and self-esteem. Informal peer tutoring is normal practice in many places around the world.

In moving from pair work to small-group work, you will be more involved in forming the groups. Heterogeneous assigned groups usually stay together to complete a task, and if they are working well may remain together for the entire unit. Groups of four to eight work well for cooperative learning tasks. Specify roles that are required. They need a leader to organize the group, to keep it on track, and to see that everyone participates; a recorder to write down the results; and a reporter to report to the class. These roles can be assigned by you or self-assigned. For a heterogeneous group, literacy level comes into play, especially for the recorder. In *LifePrints* Literacy Level, the recorder may be asked only to check items or copy words.

In managing a pair or group activity, you will find that your role changes. First, you will need to create reasons for learners to cooperate. Much of that has already been done for you in *LifePrints*. Second, you will need to move around the classroom, paying attention to what each pair or group is doing, rather than orchestrating from up front. Third, you will need to focus on what each learner in the group is doing so you can provide appropriate feedback and evaluation.

Most of the exercises and activities geared to pairs and small groups can easily be converted into one-to-one situations. In working with one learner, the tutor plays several roles: teacher, facilitator, and fellow learner. Classroom management per se is not a problem, but varying the learning situation is. The burden for performing must be shared. If learners feel they must talk all the time, their affective filter will be high. If teachers feel they must be in charge all the time, they will tire quickly. By doing exercises and conversation activities together—provided that learners have their own listening, reading, and writing time during the session—learners and tutors will set a comfortable learning/teaching pace.

IX

General Tips for Working with Literacy-Level Learners

- Know your learners and their needs. Literacy-level learners, like all adult learners, bring a wide variety of abilities, experiences, and expectations to the classroom. Factors such as educational background, health, culture, cultural views toward literacy, and personal goals can all affect the learning process. It is important to take time to assess not only learners' proficiency levels and skill needs, but also their backgrounds and goals. This helps in creating a more learner-responsive learning environment.

- Be prepared to focus awareness continually on the fact that print conveys a meaning. Make concrete the relationship between print and the actions, objects, or ideas to which it corresponds. Use gestures, pictures, or realia whenever possible to help learners clearly connect print to what it represents.

- Use oral skills as a springboard for literacy skills whenever possible, and integrate oral language and literacy as appropriate and authentic in contexts and topics.

- Create a classroom environment in which learners feel safe in practicing the language and taking risks. Literacy-level learners may have limited or negative experiences of educational settings. As a result, they may lack self-confidence in the classroom environment. Counter this by providing time for community-building activities (learner to learner and teacher to learner) and accepting "silent periods" when learners are absorbing language while they gain confidence and prepare for active production of language.

- Control the amount and level of "teacher talk" and writing. "Teacher talk" refers to all the talking that a teacher does around the actual language that is the focus of a lesson or activity. This includes directions, explanations, and general comments and conversation. Because the sheer volume of language can be overwhelming for literacy-level learners, teachers should monitor their teacher talk, keeping it simple and clear and using pictures, gestures, demonstrations, and facial expressions to reinforce their messages whenever possible. Always write distinctly in block letters, with clear spaces between letters and words, and do not overload the board with too much text.

- Help learners develop strategies for learning, and support them in self-assessment and self-evaluation of the learning process. Again, because of limited educational experiences, learners may come to the classroom without practice in the types of learning skills that foster independence in learning.

- Build structure and support into learning activities. Learners may have beginning literacy skills, but that does not mean that they do not and cannot handle complicated language functions in their everyday lives. By asking learners to fill in words in a skeletal dialogue and then create a dialogue for a similar situation, or by pre-teaching or reviewing key vocabulary before asking learners to complete a form, the teacher can make complex tasks more accessible and support learners in mastering the language they need for immediate use outside the classroom.

- Create activities that speak to different learning styles. Literacy-level learners, like all learners, have a variety of preferences for processing and learning information. Many may have been unsuccessful in traditional learning environments that rely on linguistic and mathematical skills. Activities such as song writing, poetry, making a time line, drawing a picture, TPR, or sequencing color-coded flash cards not only add variety but offer learners different ways to experience and demonstrate their mastery of language.

- Acknowledge the varied contributions learners bring to the classroom. Many literacy-level learners feel that they are working from a deficit. Draw out and incorporate into lessons the knowledge and life experiences that they have. Ask them to share their interests, and address those interests in class activities. Connect new learning to prior experiences.

- Celebrate success. At the literacy level, progress can be slow and incremental. Make sure both you and the learners have realistic expectations about outcomes, but provide regular reinforcement by showing learners that they are moving forward. This can involve creating opportunities for success in class activities, setting short-term as well as long-term goals, and helping learners recognize and acknowledge their own progress.

In going through this Teacher's Edition as you teach, note on the pages or in a notebook what worked and what didn't, and why. This will help you in teaching with *LifePrints* later on. Good luck to you and your learners.

Allene Guss Grognet
JoAnne (Jodi) Crandall
MaryAnn Cunningham Florez

Note: *In the following pages, italicized sentences generally indicate suggested questions and other language for the teacher to use. Sentences in regular type (usually in parentheses) generally indicate responses and other language that learners can be expected to produce.*

Student Performance Levels

	GENERAL LANGUAGE ABILITY	LISTENING COMPREHENSION	ORAL COMMUNICATION	BEST SCORE	CASAS SCORE
0	**LITERACY LEVEL/LEVEL ONE** No ability whatsoever.	No ability whatsoever.	No ability whatsoever.	0–8	150–170
I	**LEVEL ONE** • Functions **minimally, if at all,** in English. • Can handle only **very routine entry-level** jobs that do not require oral communication, and in which all tasks can be easily demonstrated.	• Understands only a few **isolated words, and extremely simple learned** phrases (What's your name?).	• Vocabulary limited to a few **isolated words.** • **No control** of grammar.	9–15	171–180
II	**LEVEL TWO** • Functions in a **very limited way** in situations related to **immediate needs.** • Can handle only **routine entry-level** jobs that do not require oral communication, and in which all tasks can be **easily demonstrated.**	• Understands a **limited number** of very **simple learned** phrases, spoken slowly with frequent repetitions.	• Expresses a **limited number** of **immediate** survival needs using **very simple learned phrases.** • Asks and responds to very simple learned questions.	16–28	181–190
III	• Functions **with some difficulty** in situations related to **immediate needs.** • Can handle **routine entry-level** jobs that involve only the **most basic oral communication,** and in which all tasks can be demonstrated.	• Understands **simple learned** phrases, spoken **slowly with frequent repetitions.**	• Expresses **immediate** survival needs using **simple learned phrases.** • Asks and responds to simple learned questions. • **Some control of very basic grammar.**	29–41	191–200
IV	• Can satisfy **basic survival** needs and a few **very routine social** demands. • Can handle **entry-level** jobs that involve **some simple oral** communication, but in which tasks can also be **demonstrated.**	• Understands **simple learned** phrases easily, and **some simple new** phrases containing familiar vocabulary, spoken **slowly with frequent repetitions.**	• Expresses **basic survival** needs, including asking and responding to related questions, using both **learned** and a **few new phrases.** • Participates in basic conversations in **very routine social** situations (e.g., greeting, inviting). • Speaks with **hesitation** and frequent pauses. • **Some control** of **basic** grammar.	42–50	201–210

	GENERAL LANGUAGE ABILITY	LISTENING COMPREHENSION	ORAL COMMUNICATION	BEST SCORE	CASAS SCORE
V	**LEVEL THREE** • Can satisfy **basic survival** needs and **some limited social** demands. • Can handle **jobs and job training** that involve following **simple oral** and **very basic written** instructions but in which most tasks can also be **demonstrated.**	• Understands **learned** phrases easily and **short new** phrases containing familiar vocabulary spoken slowly with **repetition.** • Has **limited** ability to understand on the telephone.	• Functions independently in most **face-to-face basic survival** situations but needs **some help.** • Asks and responds to direct questions on familiar and some unfamiliar subjects. • Still relies on **learned** phrases but also uses **new** phrases (i.e., speaks with **some creativity**) but with **hesitation** and pauses. • Communicates on the phone to express a **limited** number of **survival** needs, but with **some difficulty.** • Participates in basic conversations in a **limited number** of **social** situations. • Can occasionally clarify general meaning by simple rewording. • Increasing, but inconsistent, control of **basic grammar.**	51–57	211–220
VI	• Can satisfy **most survival needs** and **limited social** demands. • Can handle **jobs and job training** that involve following **simple oral and written** instructions and diagrams.	• Understands **conversations** containing **some unfamiliar** vocabulary on many **everyday** subjects, with a need for **repetition, rewording, or slower speech.** • Has **some** ability to understand **without face-to-face** contact (e.g, on the telephone, TV).	• Functions **independently** in most sur-vival situations, but needs **some help.** • Relies less on learned phrases; speaks with **creativity, but with hesitation.** • Communicates on the **phone** on familiar subjects, but with **some difficulty.** • Participates with **some confidence** in **social** situations when addressed **directly.** • Can sometimes **clarify** general meaning by **rewording.** • **Control** of **basic** grammar evident, but **inconsistent;** may attempt to use more difficult grammar but with almost no control.	58–64	221–235

Scope and Sequence

UNIT	FUNCTIONS	STRUCTURES	CULTURE	LIFE TASKS
Preliminary Lessons	• Expressing simple greetings • Giving personal information • Following directions • Distinguishing same and different shapes	• *What is your name?* • *My name is . . .*	Greetings and introductions Classrooms in the United States	Giving one's name in response to request Identifying one's name in print Following common classroom directions Having a simple conversation
1. Welcome to English Class	• Saying and identifying one's name • Identifying and naming common objects • Following simple directions • Identifying initial sound/letter correspondences in words	• *My name is . . .* • *Thank you.*	Classrooms in the United States	Identifying capital letters of the alphabet Writing capital letters Saying, identifying, and printing one's name Following common classroom directions
2. Personal Information	• Greeting others • Giving personal information • Identifying, saying, and writing numbers 0–5 • Identifying family members	• *I am from . . . .* • *I have . . . .* • *I am . . . .*	Use of first and last names in the United States Typical families in the United States	Greeting others using *Hello* Saying and writing first name, last name, country of origin Identifying marital status Identifying family members Describing one's own family
3. In the Neighborhood	• Identifying and naming places in the neighborhood • Identifying and interpreting signs in the neighborhood • Using numbers for addresses and telephone numbers	• *Alex lives at . . . .* • *My telephone number is . . . .* • *Help!* • *Emergency!*	Addresses in the United States Telephone numbers in the United States Emergency services in the United States Emergency telephone number (911)	Identifying places in a neighborhood Identifying and producing addresses Identifying and producing lowercase letters of the alphabet Identifying and producing numbers 0–9 Identifying and interpreting *Walk, Don't Walk, Stop, Do Not Enter, Bus Stop,* and *No Parking* signs Understanding and writing telephone numbers Using 911 emergency number

UNIT	FUNCTIONS	STRUCTURES	CULTURE	LIFE TASKS
4. Going Shopping	• Identifying and naming days of the week • Talking about money and writing monetary amounts • Identifying, saying, and writing numbers 10–49 • Identifying and naming items of food	• Questions with *when? where?* and *how much?*	Shopping for food in the United States Money in the United States	Talking about days of the week and weekly schedules Dealing with money and prices Shopping for food
5. I Am Sick	• Identifying and naming body parts • Identifying and naming symptoms or illnesses • Expressing times of the day	• *I am sick.* • *My . . . hurts.* • *I have a . . . .* • *What's wrong?* • *Can you come at . . . ?*	Making appointments Going to the doctor in the United States	Identifying body parts Calling a doctor's office and making an appointment Describing symptoms and health problems Telling time Recognizing times of the day
6. I Want a Job	• Identifying and naming jobs • Giving personal information on an application	• simple present tense verbs • *I am a . . . .*	Looking for a job in the United States	Identifying ways to find a job Looking for a job Reading job ads Completing a job application Identifying job hours and salaries

Preliminary Lessons

Summary

For adults learning English at the literacy level, the initial class meetings can be critical experiences that shape motivation, self-esteem, behavior, and even retention. The initial lessons should create an atmosphere in which learners can become familiar with the nature of the adult ESL classroom and feel at least somewhat secure in their ability to handle the content of future classes.

These preliminary lessons are designed to offer opportunities for learners to meet you, introduce themselves to each other, participate in some initial low-stress activities, and begin building a sense of community and mutual support. At the same time, there are activities that will help you learn more about learners' skills and readiness before beginning the units in the Student Book. These activities rely heavily on oral skills, often an area of strength for learners at this level, while gradually incorporating initial print elements.

Objectives

Functions

- Expressing simple greetings
- Giving personal information
- Following directions
- Distinguishing same and different shapes

Life Tasks

- Giving one's name in response to request
- Identifying one's name in print
- Following common classroom directions
- Having a simple conversation

Structures

- *What is your name?*
- *My name is . . .*

Culture

- Greetings and introductions
- Classrooms in the United States

Vocabulary

Key words:

check
circle
different
draw
match
name
read
repeat
same
say
trace
underline
write
(teacher's and learners' names)

Preliminary Lesson A

Purpose: To give practice with introductions and meeting people; to give practice in recognizing one's name as a sight word; to begin building community in the class

Teacher Preparation and Materials

1. Multicolored cards with your name and learners' names printed one per card; print name on front, a traceable outline of name on back
2. Pictures of two different people

Warm-up

1. Greet learners as they enter classroom.
2. When the class is assembled, say (pointing to yourself) *My name is . . .* Signal learners to repeat, saying *Repeat.* Repeat this several times, signaling and telling learners to repeat. Focus on the rhythm of the sentence. Walk over to one of the learners. Say, *My name is . . .* while pointing to yourself. Point to the learner and ask, *What is your name?* Repeat this activity until each learner has responded.

Presentation

1. Post pictures of two people on the board. Read the following dialogue, pointing at (or standing beside) alternating pictures to indicate a conversation. Repeat, and have learners say the conversation with you. Have one volunteer come up and say the conversation with you. Then have pairs of volunteers come up, stand beside the pictures, and say the conversation.

   PERSON 1: Hello.

   PERSON 2: Hello.

   PERSON 1: My name is _____.
     What is your name?

   PERSON 2: My name is _____.

   [When doing this with two people, shake hands.]

   PERSON 1: Nice to meet you.

   PERSON 2: Nice to meet you, too.

2. Say, *My name is . . .* Show your name card and say your name. Point to the name on the card, and say your name again.
3. Stand beside one learner and ask others to give the learner's name. When the class says the name, show the learner's name card and repeat the name. Have class repeat the name. Give the card to the learner. Repeat for each learner.

4. Have learners trace over the letters of their names on the front of the card. Have them turn the card over and trace the outlined name.

Expansion/Extension

- Collect the name cards, including your own. Mix the cards up and lay them on a desk or table. Look through the cards, find your own, and hold it up. Say your name. Have each learner come up and find his or her name card. (If you have a large class, break into smaller groups of 6–8, so that learners are not overwhelmed by the number of cards.)
- Invite learners to say and enact traditional greetings from their native countries.

Preliminary Lesson B

Purpose: To give practice in drawing shapes and in distinguishing same and different shapes

Teacher Preparation and Materials

1. Copies of Handout 1, Drawing Shapes (one copy for each learner)
2. Copies of Handout 2, Recognizing Shapes (one copy for each learner)
3. Large cutouts of shapes (two each of the shapes on Handout 1)
4. Two sets of name cards for you and learners

Warm-up

Have learners do a chain drill of their names. Put learners in a circle. Each learner says his or her own name and the names of all preceding learners.

Presentation

1. Give learners copies of Handout 1. Have learners trace the shapes. Hold up a large cutout of one shape, or draw it on the board. Ask learners to point to that shape on their copy of the handout. Repeat for all the shapes.

2. Hold up a cutout of one shape. Then hold up the second cutout of that shape. Say *same.* Put one cutout over the other. Repeat *same.* Have learners say "same." Repeat the process with several other shapes. Hold up cutout of a shape. Then hold up the cutout of a different shape. Say *different.* Put one over the other. Repeat *different.* Have learners say "different." Repeat with several other shapes. Finally, hold up a series of same and different pairs and have learners respond "same" or "different."

3. Give learners copies of Handout 2. As a class, look at the first item in each exercise. Have learners work individually to complete the exercises. Put learners in pairs to compare their answers and discuss any differences. Circulate to check accuracy and answer any questions.

4. Write your name on one side of the board; on the other side, write your name and the names of two learners. Ask learners to indicate which name on the second side is the same as the name on the first side and which names are different. Hold up pairs of cards with learners' names on them, holding up same or different names at random. Ask learners to indicate "same" or "different."

Expansion/Extension

- Lay one set of learners' name cards on a desk or table and have learners each select their own card. Then circulate with the second set and have each learner draw a card. Have learners circulate to find their matching second name card. Encourage learners to have a brief introductory conversation with the person holding their card and with the person whose card they are holding.

- Using the large cutouts of the shapes or their copies of Handout 1 as their guide, learners can circulate in the classroom and find objects that match each shape (or as many of the shapes as possible).

Preliminary Lesson C

Purpose: To give practice in following common classroom directions

Teacher Preparation and Materials

1. One set of name cards for you and learners
2. Copies of Handout 3, Following Directions, cut into cards, one set for each learner
3. Two sets of enlarged cards from Handout 3
4. *LifePrints* Student Books

Warm-up

1. As learners enter the classroom, greet each one by name and say *How are you?*
2. Have learners' name cards on desks. Learners must find their card and sit at that desk. When all learners are seated, say *How are you?* to the whole group. If anyone answers, use that response to continue modeling a conversational exchange; signal learners to repeat the response. If no one responds, supply *I am fine.* or *I'm OK.* Again model *How are you?* and signal learners to repeat. Then say the response and have them repeat. Have half the class say "How are you?" and the other half say the response. Then practice the exchange with several learners.

Presentation

1. Give each learner a set of the cards from Handout 3. First work on learner recognition of the cards. Use two enlarged individual sets of cards. Hold up a matching pair of cards (showing any direction icon). Ask *Same or different?* Repeat several times with other matching pairs. Then hold up a pair of two different cards. Ask *Same or different?* Repeat several times with other pairs of different cards.
2. Hold up a card, and ask learners to hold up the same card from their set. Repeat for each direction card.
3. Clarify the direction expressed on each card. Holding up each card in turn, demonstrate or act out the direction. Have learners imitate your action. Go through the cards again and do the action, but this time also say the direction word. Have learners repeat. Go through the cards a third time and just say the word. Have learners demonstrate the action.
4. Act out several directions and have learners name them. Hold up several cards and have learners say the direction word.

5. Put learners in pairs, each with a set of direction cards from Handout 3. One learner draws a card and demonstrates the action. The other learner says the direction word. Then the second learner draws a card and does the action, and the first learner says the word. Have learners continue alternating until they have finished with all the cards.

Expansion/Extension

Put learners in groups of three. One learner draws and shows a card, the next learner demonstrates the action, and the third learner says the word. The roles then rotate clockwise, so that the learner in each group who demonstrated the action last time now draws the card, and so on.

123456 Summary

Welcome to English Class

Objectives

Functions

- Saying and identifying one's name
- Identifying and naming common objects
- Following simple directions
- Identifying initial sound/letter correspondences in words

Life Tasks

- Identifying capital letters of the alphabet
- Writing capital letters
- Saying, identifying, and printing one's name
- Following common classroom directions

Structures

- *My name is . . .*
- *Thank you.*

Culture

- Classrooms in the United States

Vocabulary

Key words:

board
book
chair
class
English
name
paper
pen
pencil
student
teacher
welcome

Related words:

alphabet
letter
my
our
word
your

Welcome to English Class

Purpose: To give practice in greeting another person and in recognizing sight words

Teacher Preparation and Materials

1. Signs with sight words: *ENGLISH CLASS, TEACHER, STUDENTS*
2. Tape
3. Name cards with learners' names and your name printed on them

Warm-up

Greet each learner. Say *Welcome, (learner's name)*, as each one enters the class. When learners are seated, repeat the Welcome greeting to the whole class.

Presentation

1. Have learners turn to page 5 and look at the picture. Encourage and reinforce any identification of items in the picture that is expressed.

2. Point to the picture and say *Welcome to English class*. Ask learners *What is this? Where are they?* Use gestures to convey the question, and point at the picture. If no one responds, say *English class*. Repeat. Have learners repeat.

3. Hold up the sign with *ENGLISH CLASS* printed on it. Ask learners to find that sign in the picture. Ask learners where to place the sign in your classroom. Use gestures as needed to convey the question. Tape the sign to the classroom door, as in the picture. Point to the classroom and to the words on the sign, and say *English class*. Repeat. Have learners repeat.

4. Point to the teacher in the picture. Ask learners who it is. If no one responds, say *teacher*. Repeat *teacher*. Hold up the sign with *TEACHER* on it. Repeat, pointing to the word on the sign. Then point to the students in the picture. Ask learners to identify them. If no one responds, say *students*. Repeat. Hold up the sign with *STUDENTS* on it. Repeat, pointing to the word on the sign.

5. Hold up the *TEACHER* sign. Say the word. Ask learners to indicate the teacher

WELCOME TO ENGLISH CLASS.

in their classroom. Tape the sign to your clothes. Repeat the process with the *STUDENTS* sign. Place it on a desk in front of all students.

6. Pass out the name cards. Write a chart on the board that says *ENGLISH CLASS* at the top and has two columns underneath, headed *TEACHER* and *STUDENTS*. Have learners tape their name cards under the appropriate heading. Tape your name card under *TEACHER*.

Expansion/Extension

- Have learners label the teacher and students on the picture in their books.
- You may wish to have learners give the words for teacher and students in their native language and teach others in the class how to say the words.

Welcome

Purpose: To give practice in understanding a simple story and in matching words with pictures

Teacher Preparation and Materials

1. ▭▭ Audiotape for Literacy Level
2. Copies of Handout 4, Strip Story, cut into strips, one set for every two learners
3. Signs with sight words: *ENGLISH CLASS, WELCOME, THANK YOU,* and *NAME*
4. Signs with sight words: *STUDENT* and *TEACHER,* with strings to hang signs around the neck, one set for every two learners *(Expansion/Extension)*

Warm-up

Have learners look at the picture on page 5. Point to the teacher in the picture and ask *Who is this?* Point to the students and ask *Who are they?* Ask *Where are they?* Have learners respond as a group and individually.

Presentation

1. Have learners turn to page 6 and look at the pictures. Point to the teacher and ask *Who is this?* Point to the student and ask *Who is this?* Ask *Where are they?* Elicit group and individual responses.

2. Direct learners to look at the words on the page. Hold up the sign with *ENGLISH CLASS.* Ask learners to find and underline those words on the page.

3. ▭▭ Play the audiotape. Point to the corresponding pictures as learners listen. ▭▭ Play the story again and have learners point to the corresponding pictures.

4. Point to the picture of Susan. Ask *Who is Susan?* Hold up the *TEACHER* and *STUDENT* signs, and ask *Teacher or student?* Elicit responses from several learners. Point to the picture of Alex. Ask *Who is Alex?* and elicit responses.

5. Hold up the signs with *WELCOME, NAME,* and *THANK YOU.* Say the words while pointing to the signs. Have learners find the words on the page and circle them.

6. Put learners in pairs and give each pair a set of strips from Handout 4. Have the pairs put the strip story in order.

Expansion/Extension

- Cut apart the words and pictures on the strip story strips. Have learners, in pairs, match pictures and captions and put the story in order. Have pairs recite the story or tape strips in order on the board.

- With a volunteer, act out the conversation. Put learners in pairs and give each pair a *TEACHER* and a *STUDENT* sign. Have pairs enact the story. Then have them repeat, switching roles.

Letters

Purpose: To introduce capital letters

Teacher Preparation and Materials

1. Cards or pieces of paper with traceable outlines of your name and learners' names, one for each learner

2. Name cards with traceable outlines of the first and last names of each learner *(Expansion/Extension)*

Warm-up

Ask several learners for their names. Print the names on the board. Say the names while pointing to them. Indicate all the names and ask *What are these?* Elicit or say *names.* Repeat, and have learners repeat.

Presentation

1. Have learners turn to page 7. Point to the picture of the teacher. Ask *What is her name?* Say *Susan,* and write it on the board. Point to the name on the page. Say *Her name is Susan.* Repeat. Have learners say the name. Point to the individual letters of the name on the board and spell the name.

2. Repeat the procedure with Alex.

3. Point to the names *SUSAN* and *ALEX* on the board. Say, *What are these?* Elicit or say *names.* Repeat *names.* Point to learners' names written on the board. Ask *What are these?* Elicit the word *names.*

4. Pass out the cards or papers with traceable outlines of your name and individual learners' names. Write your name on the board. Point to it and say *My name is . . .* Spell your name, pointing to individual letters and tracing them. Spell it again, having learners trace each letter as it is said. Ask one learner *What is your name?* Point to the outline of the learner's name on the card or paper. Repeat with another learner. Have all learners trace their names on their papers.

5. Write several names (*ALEX, SUSAN,* your name, a few learners' names) and several individual letters on the board. Point to the names and ask, *What are these?* Elicit or say *names.* Point to the letters and say *letters.* Again point to the names and say

names. Point to individual letters in the names and say *letters.*

6. Point to names and letters randomly, and have learners indicate which you are pointing to.

Expansion/Extension

Supply learners with name cards with their first and last names on them. Have them trace both names and say them.

The Alphabet

Purpose: To introduce and give practice in naming and writing the letters of the alphabet

Teacher Preparation and Materials

1. Complete alphabet, printed on the board or chart paper
2. ▆▆ Audiotape for Literacy Level
3. Copies of Handout 9, Letter Cards (Capitals), cut into cards or sets of flash cards with one capital letter on each card (three to five sets, depending on class size)
4. Blank pieces of paper
5. A ball, beanbag, or similar item to throw

Warm-up

1. Write several letters and names on the board. Point to a letter or a name, and have learners identify which it is.
2. Show the whole alphabet on the board or chart paper. Ask *Letters or names?* Ask learners to say the names of any letters that they know.

Presentation

1. Present the whole alphabet again. ▆▆ Play the audiotape and point to each letter as it is named. ▆▆ Play the audiotape again, having learners say the name of each letter along with the tape. Repeat as needed. Go over the names of the letters again without the tape, pointing to each letter on the page or on the alphabet written on the board. If necessary, give learners more time between letters to say the name of the letter.
2. Break one set of alphabet cards into groups of five or six letters. Put learners in groups of three or four. Give each group a set of letter cards. Have groups identify and practice saying the letters on their cards. Circulate and assist as they do this. Bring the groups together. Beginning with the group that has *A, B, C, D, E,* have each group recite its letters aloud. When they have completed the alphabet, have groups exchange cards, practice a new set of letters, and recite. Repeat until all learners have said the complete alphabet.

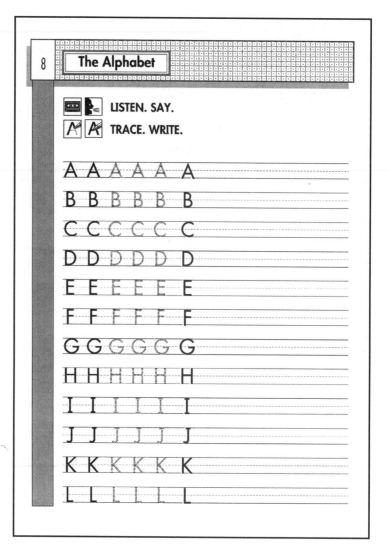

3. Present the alphabet as the *ABC* song. Have learners clap quietly for each letter as it is sung, to be sure they can distinguish the name of one letter from another. Repeat as necessary. Repeat the song, breaking it into sets of letters, following the rhythm of the song. Alternate with the learners saying sets of letters. For example, you sing *A, B,* and learners respond *C, D,* alternating until the alphabet is completed. Sing the complete song with learners. This can be repeated in future lessons to review and reinforce the names of the letters.
4. Distribute alphabet cards, one to a learner. (Distribute duplicates if there are more than 26 learners.) Call out a letter; the learner with that letter must stand. Model with several volunteers.
5. Hold up cards with letters and have learners name the letter.
6. Have learners look at page 8. Point to the first letter and name it. Have learners repeat and trace the outlines. Then have them write one example of the letter freehand. Repeat for each letter. When finished, have learners go back and write each letter again, twice, working

individually. If learners complete the task quickly, have them work in pairs with flash cards. One draws a series of five letters and names them. The second writes the letters. Learners check their work by comparing the letters written and those on the cards. They then switch roles.

7. Put some sight words already covered on the board (FOR EXAMPLE: *STUDENT, ENGLISH, CLASS, WELCOME, NAME, TEACHER*). Spell each word, pointing to each letter as it is named. Ask learners to spell the words as you point to the letters.

Expansion/Extension

Note: The expansion/extension ideas here can be used with this lesson or incorporated in future lessons to review and reinforce the alphabet.

- Have learners, as a class, create a large alphabet strip (or several created by groups, if the class is large) to hang in the room. (Leave room between letters so that lower-case letters can be added later.)

- Have each learner choose a letter and write it in the middle of a piece of paper. Then have learners look for and cut out examples of their letters from magazines, newspapers, and so on, and paste them on the paper. When learners finish, the individual pages can be assembled as a class alphabet book.

- Hold up two different letter cards. Say the name of one of the letters. Have learners point to the one you are saying.

- Produce additional sets of the alphabet cards. Put learners in groups of three or four and give each group two complete sets of cards. Have them mix the cards and lay them face down on a table. Learners then take turns playing a Concentration game to find the matches.

- Place a pile of the alphabet cards on the table. Call out a letter and have learners find the card. (This can be done individually, with each learner having a pile, or in pairs or groups who work together with one pile.)

- Have learners stand in a circle. Say the letter *A,* and throw a ball or beanbag to a learner. The learner says *B* and throws the ball to another learner, anywhere in the circle. The second learner says *C,* and the process continues until the alphabet,

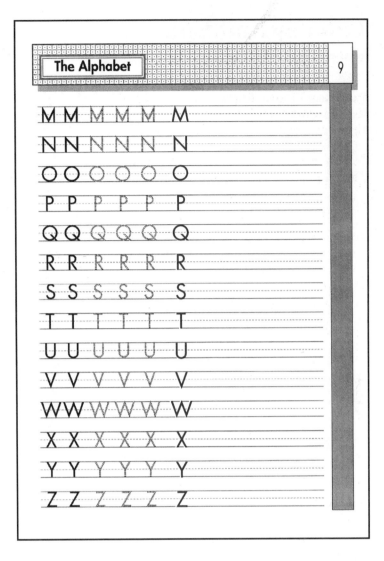

or the portion you want to practice, is completed. This can be repeated periodically for review. You can also start the process with any other letter of the alphabet and have learners continue from that point.

- Have learners look at signs or labels in the classroom. Point to capital letters on the signs and labels, and have learners say the name of the letter you point to.

- Give learners a page with simple text printed in capital letters (FOR EXAMPLE: an ad or a flyer), or have them turn to a completed page in the Student Book. Ask learners to find certain letters on the page. FOR EXAMPLE: As them to circle all the *A*s, underline all the *M*s, check all the *O*s, and so on.

- As learners progress through the Student Book lessons, have them write or copy vocabulary words to create word banks or flash cards, rather than giving them preprinted ones. Ask them to spell vocabulary words for a lesson as they look at them, to reinforce letter recognition (not as a spelling exercise).

Letters and Sounds

Purpose: To give practice in identifying initial sounds and letters in words; to give practice in matching oral and written versions of sight words

Teacher Preparation and Materials

1. Learners' name cards
   (Expansion/Extension)
2. 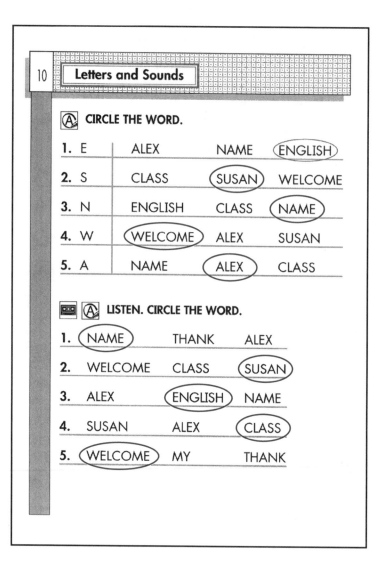 Audiotape for Literacy Level

Warm-up

1. Put a list of previously studied sight words on the board. (FOR EXAMPLE: *NAME, CIRCLE, STUDENT, TEACHER, WELCOME, UNDERLINE, ALEX, SUSAN*) Point to each word; ask learners to read the word and act it out or point to it (in the classroom or a picture).

2. Point to each word and pronounce it. Underline the first letter of the first word and ask learners to name it. Repeat the word, exaggerating the initial sound. Point to the first letter. Ask learners to name the letter. Then ask them to reproduce the sound. Repeat for each word.

3. Ask learners to identify a word on the board that starts with an *S*, a *T*, and so on. Name all initial letters of the sight words on the board.

Presentation

1. Have learners turn to page 10. Look at the first item in the top exercise. Write *E* and *ENGLISH*. Point to the circle in the book around *ENGLISH*. Ask *Why?* Write *E* again, and then use it to continue writing *ENGLISH*.

2. Have learners complete the exercise individually. Review the answers. Have volunteers explain their responses, following the model for *ENGLISH* used in step 1.

3. Write *STUDENT* and *TEACHER* on the board. Say *student* and ask learners to indicate which word it is. Repeat with *teacher*. Play the audiotape, and have learners complete the second exercise. Review answers together. Write the answers on the board so that learners know which word they should have underlined.

Expansion/Extension

- Pass out learners' name cards or have learners find their own. Have learners line up alphabetically according to the first letter in their names. Have each learner say the first letter of his or her name and then say the name.

- Write the alphabet in capital letters on the board or on chart paper. Have learners write your name and each learner's name under the letter with which it starts.

What Is Your Name?

Purpose: To give practice in writing and spelling names

Teacher Preparation and Materials

1. Copies of Handout 5, Student Interview Chart, one for each learner
2. Learners' name cards
3. Blank chart paper *(Expansion/Extension)*
4. Sets of flash cards with letters of alphabet (four or five sets, depending on size of class)
5. Blank name tags *(Expansion/Extension)*

Warm-up

1. Put learners in groups. Give each group a set of alphabet flash cards. Have groups put the cards in alphabetical order.
2. Spell several of the sight words learned to date (FOR EXAMPLE: *student, English, class, name, teacher*). Have learners write the word that you spell and then say it.

Presentation

1. On the board, write *My name is . . .* (complete with your name). Ask learners *What is my name?* When they respond, spell the name and write it on the board again. Ask learners to spell the name.

2. Have learners turn to page 11. Point to the picture of the teacher. Ask *Who is she?* Elicit the name. Point to the name on the page and say it. Write *SUSAN* on the board; spell *S-U-S-A-N*, pointing to the letters as you say each one. Then ask learners to spell *Susan*. Read *My name is Susan.* Have learners read the sentence. Repeat the steps with Alex.

3. Ask learners to read the last line on the page. Confirm that it is *My name is _____*. Have learners write their names on the line in the book. They can use their name cards as reference, if necessary. Then have each learner in turn read the last sentence with his or her name.

4. Have learners turn to a partner and spell their names. The partner writes the name. Then they reverse roles. Learners then check what their partners wrote.

5. Give each learner a copy of Handout 5. Have them use the chart to record the

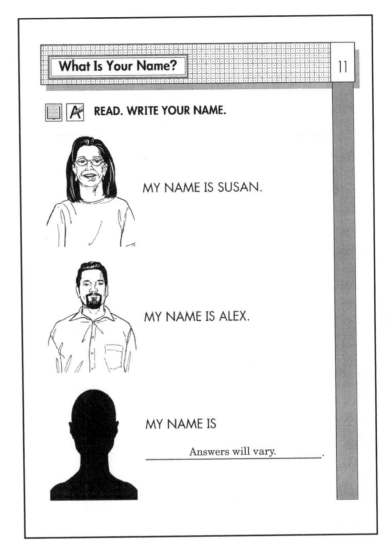

names of up to eight classmates. Learners circulate, ask classmates to spell their names, and write what is spelled.

Expansion/Extension

- Have learners create their own name tags to wear. Have them write their names and then decorate the tags as they wish.
- Create a class poster entitled *OUR ENGLISH CLASS.* Have learners write their own names on the poster and decorate it.
- Have learners ask three to five people outside the class to spell their names as learners record the names in their notebooks. Have them report on the names to the class.

English Class

Purpose: To give practice in reading and writing words for common classroom objects; to give practice in spelling words

Teacher Preparation and Materials

1. Large cards with sight words: *PEN, PENCIL, STUDENT, PAPER, BOOK, TEACHER, BOARD*
2. Blank large index cards
3. Blank signs or pieces of paper
4. Tape

Warm-up

1. On the board, write a series of broken lines for each letter of sight words *pen, pencil, student, paper, book, teacher, board* (_ _ _ _ for *book*, _ _ _ for *pen*, and so on). Have learners copy the lines. Then dictate the spelling of the words, and have learners write the letters on the lines. After the first word, confirm that learners are writing the letters correctly. When all words have been spelled, call on volunteers to fill in the letters on the board and correct as a group.
2. Point to and say each word on the board. Have learners repeat the word. Ask if they know any of the words, and if so, to point to the object it names. If any learners identify words, give them the sign with the word on it and have them tape it to the object. Have learners guess the remaining objects, giving hints as necessary, and tape signs to them.

Presentation

1. Have learners turn to page 12. Have them write the words for the objects in the picture, using the signs for reference. Then have them chorally say the words for those objects.
2. Point to labeled objects in the classroom or in the picture. Have learners individually say the words for the objects.
3. Have learners create their own vocabulary flash cards. Distribute large index cards. Have learners draw a picture of the object on the front and print the word on the reverse. Then in pairs, have learners quiz each other using the cards.

4. Have learners point out other things in the room that they can name or want named. Have them create a sign for the object and also create a flash card for it. Try to include the words *CHAIR* and *DESK*.

Expansion/Extension

- Learners can begin to create their own vocabulary notebooks with words and pictures, or the class can begin creating a class vocabulary notebook or list.
- Have learners visit other classrooms and list what they see in them.
- Have learners draw and label classrooms from their native countries.

In English Class

Purpose: To give practice in identifying initial letters in words; to give practice in matching words and pictures or objects

Teacher Preparation and Materials

Learner-created vocabulary cards *(Expansion/Extension)*

Warm-up

1. Spell five or six of the vocabulary words from page 12. Have learners write them, and in pairs compare and check what they have written.

2. Say the words, emphasizing the initial sound. Have learners name the first letter of each word.

Presentation

1. Have learners turn to page 13 and complete the first exercise. Review answers together. In each item, say the word, emphasizing the initial sound. Have learners say or point to the letter they circled for each. Write the letter on the board for learners to check their work. Say the word again, and have learners repeat.

2. After reviewing all items, look again at the letters on the board. Name the letters again, and say the initial sound it represents in this exercise. Ask learners to say the name of the letter and the sound for each one.

3. Say the following groups of words from Unit 1 lessons (or words that learners are likely to have heard in the lessons). Have learners write the letter for the sound they hear at the beginning of the words in each group: *pen, pencil, paper; board, book; Susan, student, stand; name, no.* Include any learners' or teacher's names that start with the same letters as other words from the lessons. Emphasize initial sounds if necessary.

4. Have learners complete the second exercise, matching vocabulary words and pictures. Review answers as a group.

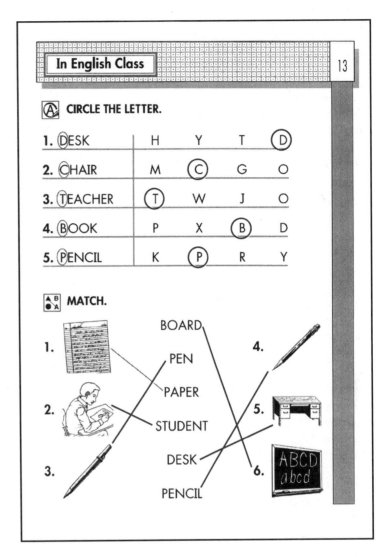

Expansion/Extension

- Have groups or pairs of learners use their vocabulary cards (for words in the unit and any additional classroom objects for which they created cards) to do a matching game, matching the word with the picture for each object.

- Hold up pictures of vocabulary words, using a learner's set of cards, and ask learners to name the object. Then ask them to name the first letter and demonstrate the sound it represents.

- Ask learners to brainstorm any other words that they have learned in this unit (FOR EXAMPLE: *hello, welcome, English*) and practice the initial sounds.

- Say groups of words that are unfamiliar to learners but that have initial letters like those of words in this lesson (*P, S, N, B, T, W, D,* etc.). Have learners write the letter that corresponds to each sound.

My Class

Purpose: To review vocabulary from the unit; to give practice in talking and writing about classrooms

Teacher Preparation and Materials

1. Learners' name cards
2. Blank pieces of chart paper
3. Learners' vocabulary cards and signs for classroom objects
4. Tape *(Expansion/Extension)*
5. A blank grid like the one on page 14, on board or chart paper *(Expansion/Extension)*

Warm-up

Ask learners to write their names on pieces of paper, without looking at their name cards or the Student Book pages. When they finish writing, have them compare what they wrote with their name cards. Help them correct any mistakes, and then write the names again, if necessary.

Presentation

1. Have learners turn to page 14. Explain that together you will be writing about "our class" (students, teacher, things in the room). Have learners say your name, spell it for them (or have a learner spell it if possible), and then have learners write the name on the page. Have learners write their own names on the page also.

2. As a group, look at the pictures in the second exercise. Discuss if the item in each picture is in the classroom. Show learners how to check yes or no on the chart based on the discussion. Have learners complete the spelling of the words individually. Then ask volunteers to write the complete words on the board for learners to check their work.

3. Have learners brainstorm any other objects in the classroom and write them on the board. Learners can copy the words in their books.

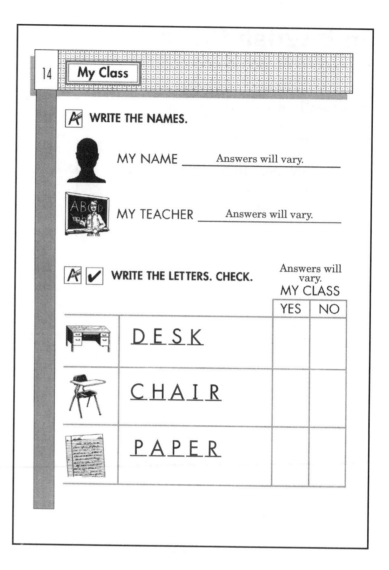

Expansion/Extension

- Hold a class poster contest. Explain that learners can use the information from the Student Book page to create a poster with the theme "Our Class." Divide the class into groups of three or four. You may wish to create your own poster as a model.

- Hang all posters in the classroom. Have learners vote on which poster or posters will hang permanently on the door of the classroom. Label each poster with a letter. Give learners ballots with all the letters and ask them to place a check beside their choice.

- Have learners copy a blank grid like the one on page 14. Have them complete a new grid about a classroom in their native country. Encourage them to report to the class the differences and similarities between their former and current classrooms.

123456 Summary
Personal Information

Objectives

Functions

- Greeting others
- Giving personal information
- Identifying, saying, and writing numbers 0–5
- Identifying family members

Life Tasks

- Greeting others using *Hello*
- Saying and writing first name, last name, country of origin
- Identifying marital status
- Identifying family members
- Describing one's own family

Structures

- *I am from . . .*
- *I have . . .*
- *I am . . .*

Culture

- Use of first and last names in the United States
- Typical families in the United States

Vocabulary

Key words:

am
brother
children
daughter
family
father
have
hello
husband
married
mother
number
parents
single
sister
son
wife

Related words:

aunt
'bye
cousin
goodbye
hi
uncle

Personal Information

Purpose: To introduce and give practice with basic greetings

Teacher Preparation and Materials

1.  Audiotape for Literacy Level
2. Stack of large blank white cards or signs

Warm-up

1. As learners enter the classroom, welcome them with various greetings (FOR EXAMPLE: *Hi, Hello, Good morning, Good evening*). When the class is assembled, ask learners to say the various greetings used (and brainstorm any others, if they can).

2. Spell the greetings, and have learners write them. Write the greetings on the board so learners can check what they wrote. Say each one again, pointing to it. Have learners repeat.

Presentation

1. Have learners look at page 15. Ask them to describe what is happening. Ask learners to find and then circle or underline the word *Hello* on the page. Make sure they find it twice.

2. Play the audiotape, and have learners listen to the conversation. Repeat if necessary. Have learners repeat the conversation. Point to the characters' hands in the picture. Ask what the characters are doing.

3. Ask a volunteer to come to the front. Walk out of the classroom and re-enter, role-playing a greeting with the volunteer. Have several pairs of learners do a role play in the same way. Record the words or sentences from the role plays (including the first one that you did) on blank cards or signs and tape them randomly to the board. Have volunteers come forward, choose a greeting and a response to it, say the response aloud, and tape the cards to the board as a pair.

4. Have learners use greetings in a chain activity. One learner greets another, who responds appropriately; they may shake hands or use another gesture of greeting (such as a wave). The second learner turns to a third and greets that person, who also

responds, and so on. Learners can use any appropriate greeting and response.

Expansion/Extension

- Demonstrate a person taking leave of another person. Have learners brainstorm appropriate words or phrases and responses. Pronounce each and have learners repeat. Spell the words for the learners and have them write what you say. Pairs of learners can role-play leave-taking exchanges.

- Have learners practice introductory conversations from earlier lessons (such as on pages 5 or 6), adding suitable greetings and leave-takings.

Names and Introductions

Purpose: To give practice in giving one's name and the name of one's native country

Teacher Preparation and Materials

1.  Audiotape for Literacy Level
2. Cards with different ways forms might ask for a person's name *(Expansion/Extension)* FOR EXAMPLE:

NAME _____ ; NAME _____
       FIRST   LAST

3. Globe or map of the world

Warm-up

Have learners review introductions with a chain activity. One learner says to another *Hello. My name is . . .* The other responds appropriately and gives his or her name.

Presentation

1. Play the audiotape of the first four sentences on page 16. Repeat if necessary. Say each sentence and have learners repeat it chorally. Ask them to identify any words they don't know.
2. Draw two columns on the board, labeled *FIRST NAME* and *LAST NAME*. Write *MY NAME IS ALEX MARCOS.* Then write Alex's first and last names in the appropriate columns. Say *My name is . . .* and give your own first and last name. Write your first and last names on the board. Ask learners in which columns you should write each name.
3. Have learners write *MY NAME IS . . .* on separate paper. If any have trouble with their last name, write it for them and have them copy and practice. Then have learners come forward and write their first and last names in the appropriate columns.
4. Model this conversation:
   What is your name?
   My name is . . . My first name is . . .
   My last name is . . .
   Can you spell your name?
   Have learners circulate, say the conversation with classmates, and write the first and last names of three other learners.

5. Have learners look at the next line on the page. Play the audiotape. Have learners repeat. Ask them what Alex's country is (Mexico). Using the world map or globe, have learners find their native country and say and write the sentence about themselves. Help with spelling of country names.
6. Play the audiotape for the page again. Have learners complete the exercise at the bottom of the page.

Expansion/Extension

Put learners in groups of three. Give each group a card with one of the ways a form might ask for names. Let each group choose the name of a group member and write it on the card. Have a volunteer from each group put that group's answer on the board.

Personal Information

Purpose: To give practice in giving personal information; to give practice in distinguishing letters, words, and numerals

Teacher Preparation and Materials

1. █▀█ Audiotape for Literacy Level
2. Beachball, beanbag, or similar object to toss
3. World map
4. Pictures to illustrate *married* and *single* (FOR EXAMPLE: an adult alone, a couple getting married)

Warm-up

Toss a beachball, beanbag, or similar object to a learner and ask *Where are you from?* The learner answers and tosses the ball to another learner, asking the same question. Continue until all learners have asked and answered the question.

Presentation

1. Ask learners to look at the first three lines of the story on page 17 and to indicate what looks the same or different from Alex's story on page 16. Have them look at the picture. Ask *Who is it?* Have them write the new first and last names on the lines.

2. Ask learners to look at the next picture and sentence. Ask where Susan is from. If no one responds, say *United States.* Have learners repeat. Ask learners to underline the words *UNITED STATES.* Confirm. Have them find the United States on the world map.

3. Ask learners to look at the next picture and describe what they see. Elicit or give an explanation of *married* (FOR EXAMPLE: point to a wedding ring, show a picture of a wedding). Ask each learner *Are you married?* The first time a learner answers *No,* introduce the word *single.* Hold up pictures and ask learners to indicate *single* or *married* for each one. Ask the remaining learners *Are you single or married?*

4. Write on the board *I HAVE 2 CHILDREN.* Have learners look at the next picture and point to Susan. Point to the children and indicate that they are Susan's. Read the

sentence on the board, holding up two fingers when the number is said. Point to the children in the picture when the word is said.

5. █▀█ Play the audiotape; have learners listen and follow on the page.

Expansion/Extension

- Write on the board several letters, one or two words, and the number 2. Identify each as letter, word, or number. Have learners repeat. Put other letters, words, and numbers on the board, and have learners indicate which is which.

- Have learners find examples of letters, words, and numbers outside of class and report their findings to the class.

Numbers 0–5

Purpose: To give practice in writing numbers 0–5 and counting 0–5

Teacher Preparation and Materials

1. Pictures of varying numbers (1–5) of children

2. Varying numbers (1–5) of small objects that can be counted in class (FOR EXAMPLE: pencils, paper clips, chalk, coins, keys) *(Expansion/Extension)*

Warm-up

1. Review *children.* Show pictures and ask *Who are they?* Elicit *children.* Show a picture of one child; say *child,* and have learners repeat.

2. Have learners look at the pictures at the top of page 18. Have them identify the woman in the picture on the left as Susan. Show them that the woman in the picture on the right is in Susan's class. Point her out in the picture on page 5.

Presentation

1. Have learners look again at the pictures at the top of the page. Ask them to read the sentence under the picture on the left. Point to the children in the picture and say *Children. Two children.* Point to one child and then the other. Hold up two fingers and say *Two children.* Have learners repeat and also hold up two fingers. Ask *How many children?* using intonation and body language to indicate a question. Give the answer *Two children.* Repeat the question and answer, signaling learners to say it with you. Then ask the question and elicit the answer.

2. On the board, draw a line and write *CHILDREN* next to it. Draw another line and write *CHILD* next to it. Point to the words and ask *Same or different?* Point to the word *CHILDREN* in the Student Book; ask *How many children?* When learners say *Two,* write the number on the line in front of *CHILDREN.* Point to the word *CHILD* on the board and ask them to point to it in the book. Ask *How many? What number is it?* Have them point to the number 1. Say *One. One child.* and

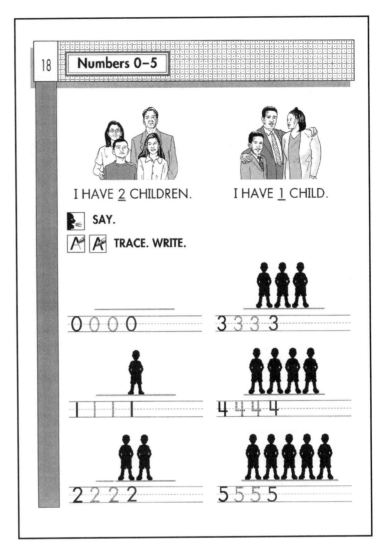

hold up one finger. Have learners repeat. Write the number 1 on the line in front of *CHILD.*

3. Point to the empty picture and ask *How many children? Two children?* When learners indicate no, say *No children.* Point to the numeral and say *Zero children.* Repeat, and have learners repeat. Have learners trace and then write the zero. Repeat this process for each of the pictures and the corresponding numerals in the exercise.

Expansion/Extension

Arrange small objects (paper clips, pencils, coins, etc.) in groups of one to five on a table. Have learners count the objects and record the number of each. Elicit or give the word for each object. Have learners say and then write the number and word for each (FOR EXAMPLE: two pencils, five paper clips).

Practicing Numbers 0–5

Purpose: To give practice in matching numbers to amounts; to give practice in recognizing written and oral forms of numbers

Teacher Preparation and Materials

1. Blank paper for dictation
2. ▬▬ Audiotape for Literacy Level
3. Copies of Handout 6, Number Cards (0–5) or pieces of paper with a number on each (enough so that each learner will have one number)

Warm-up

1. Have learners count off from 0 to 5, holding up the correct number of fingers for the number they say. When they reach 5, have the next person start again with 0.
2. Hold up number cards 0 to 5 at random. Have learners call out the number.

Presentation

1. Have learners look at page 19 and complete the first exercise. Have learners turn to the person next to (or behind) them, exchange books, and correct each other's answers. Ask the class to say the numbers between 0 and 5 that are not used in the exercise (0 and 1). Have two volunteers come to the board to illustrate and write the two numbers.
2. Put learners in pairs. Ask one to dictate the contents of the pictures in exercise 1 (5 children, 4 children, and so on). The other learner writes the numbers and words. When the first learner is finished, the two switch roles. When they finish, have them compare their written answers.
3. Give each learner a piece of paper with a number from 0 to 5 on it. Have them write their number on the top of the paper, then move around the room to find other learners with the same number, and record the names on their sheet of paper.
4. ▬▬ Play the audiotape, and have learners complete exercise 2. Go over responses as a class.

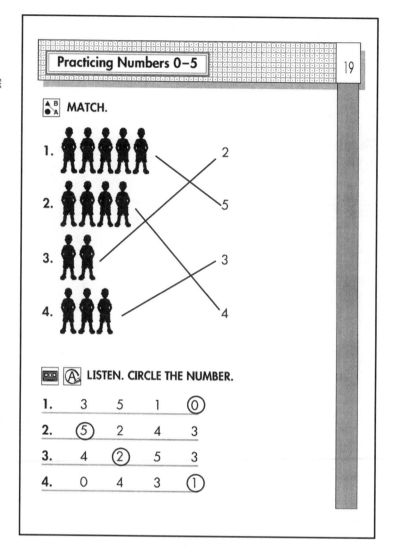

Expansion/Extension

- Ask learners to write the numbers 1 to 5 down the left side of a piece of paper. Model this on the board. Write the words *yes* and *no* on the board after each number. Have learners do the same on their own paper. Using objects for which learners know the words, show various groups of objects and say *I have (a certain number of)* . . . Ask learners to circle *yes* or *no* on their papers. FOR EXAMPLE: Holding up two student name cards, say *Number one. I have four names. Yes or no?* When finished, go over the answers as a class.

- Have learners keep a record (FOR EXAMPLE: with pictures) of where they hear or see the numbers 0 to 5 during one day and report the results to class.

The Family

Purpose: To introduce words for family members

Teacher Preparation and Materials

A picture of a family (your own or from a book or magazine)

Warm-up

Show a picture of a family. Make sure it has at least one set of parents and a child or children. Ask learners to describe what they see and identify any family members for whom they know the words already. If the picture shows your family, share the names of the family members.

Presentation

1. Have learners turn to page 20 and look at the first picture. Point to Susan and ask them to identify her. Point to the group in the picture, and indicate that this is Susan's family. Point to each member of the group, and give the person's name (*Her name is Susan. His name is Jim.* and so on). Say *family,* and have learners repeat. Ask learners to spell *family* as you point to each letter. Have learners copy the word on the line under the word.

2. Repeat the process with the other pictures and words. For the picture of Susan and her husband, be sure to ask *Are they married?* For the picture of the children, ask *How many children?*

3. Put two columns on the board, one labeled *PARENTS* and the other labeled *CHILDREN.* Have learners copy this. Ask them to list the names of Susan's family members under the correct heading.

4. Ask learners *Who is Susan?* Prompt as necessary to help learners identify Susan's roles in the family based on the information on this page (parent, wife). Do the same with the other family members. Distinguish *parents (How many? Two parents)* and *parent (How many? One parent).*

Expansion/Extension

- Ask learners to draw a picture of a typical family in their native countries and what they consider a typical family in the United States. Discuss the similarities and differences.

- Learners may want to draw pictures or bring in photos of their own families and talk about who they are and what their roles are. Some learners, however, may not have photos of their family or may find the subject painful.

Members of the Family

Purpose: To introduce additional words for family members; to give practice in using words for family members

Teacher Preparation and Materials

1. Copies of Handout 7, My Family (one for each learner)
2. A picture of a family (four people or more)

Warm-up

Show the picture of a family (husband, wife, at least two children) and ask learners to identify family members when you point to them. Elicit all the words learned in the previous lesson. Then point to pairs (husband/wife, parents/children) and have learners identify the words specific to the relationship being shown. Point to the children and ask if anyone knows what the words are for those relationships. If learners know *brother* and *sister,* use those words to move forward to the material on the Student Book page. If not, supply the words.

Presentation

1. Have learners turn to page 21 and look at the first picture. Point to Susan, and ask learners to identify her role (parent). Point to the children, and elicit their role in the family (children). Point to Susan and then to the children to indicate the relationship specifically between them. Read the first word, *mother.* Repeat, and have learners say the word. Ask learners to spell the word as you point to each letter. Have learners copy the word on the line underneath. Point to Susan again and say *Susan is their mother,* again indicating the relationship is directly between Susan and the children. Repeat the process with each word and each picture.

2. Call out random words from the vocabulary studied to this point in the Student Book. Include words for members of the family (*mother, family, brother,* and so on). Instruct learners that if they hear a word for a member of the family, they stand up. If a word is not a family member term, they sit down.

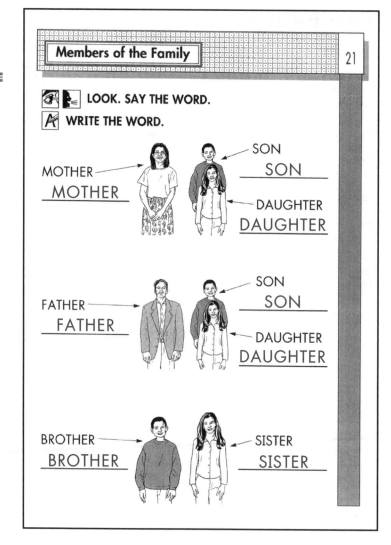

3. Write the names of Susan and her family on the board (*SUSAN, JIM, NICK, LISA*). Ask learners to copy the names onto a sheet of paper. Have learners write all the roles each person plays in the family under the person's name. (FOR EXAMPLE: Under *SUSAN* learners could write *wife, mother, parent.*) Prompt as necessary, saying, for example, *Susan is a . . .* or *Is Susan a . . . ?* When finished, have learners work in pairs and compare their answers.

4. Give each learner a copy of Handout 7, and have them complete it with information about their own families.

Expansion/Extension

Introduce words for other family members, using the terms learned as points of reference (FOR EXAMPLE: *uncle* = brother of your mother.) Draw a family tree to illustrate.

Brothers and Sisters

Purpose: To give practice in describing one's family; to introduce regular plurals

Teacher Preparation and Materials

1. A picture of your family (or a picture from a book or magazine)
2. A simple description of your family, written on chart paper *(Expansion/Extension)*

Warm-up

Show the picture of your family. Ask learners to identify the members as you point to them. (FOR EXAMPLE: father, daughter, children) Then ask questions with *How many* about the members. FOR EXAMPLE: *How many parents? How many mothers? How many sons?* Give a simple oral description of your family. (FOR EXAMPLE: *This is my family. I have one mother. I have two sisters.* and so on.)

Presentation

1. Have learners turn to page 22 and look at the picture of Alex. Ask them to identify him. Have the class read the first sentence under the picture. Remind learners of what *single* means. Ask the class (or a volunteer) to read the next sentence, filling in the blank with an appropriate number (0). Prompt if necessary to elicit the number.

2. Have learners look at the next picture and identify Alex. Ask who is in the picture overall (Alex's family). Ask learners to identify Alex's roles in the family (son, brother) and the roles of the others in the picture. Have them complete the sentences below the picture.

3. Draw a representation of Alex's family on the board, using stick figures or something similarly simple. Label one of the children *ALEX*. Write *I HAVE 2 BROTHERS* under the picture. Draw another family, this one with two female children and one male child. Label one of the children *SUSAN*. Write *I HAVE 1 BROTHER* under this picture. Present each family and read the sentence under it; emphasize the final *-s* on the plural. Learners repeat. Point to *BROTHER* and *BROTHERS*. Ask learners what is different in the two. When the final *-s* on *brothers* is indicated, have them guess why it is different.

Remind them they have seen the use of *-s* for plurals in *parent* and *parents*.

Expansion/Extension

Say the description of your family again. Ask learners to listen and write the words for family members and the number of members. Present the written description. Have learners come forward and underline the numbers and members, then compare with what they wrote.

Words and Sounds

Purpose: To give practice in linking sounds to letters; to give practice in categorizing words for family members

Teacher Preparation and Materials

1. Beachball, beanbag, or similar object to toss
2. Pictures of individual men and women
3. ▄▄▄ Audiotape for Literacy Level

Warm-up

1. Begin a chain activity by saying something about your family (FOR EXAMPLE: *I have one mother*). Toss the ball to a learner, who has to say something true about his or her family (FOR EXAMPLE: *I have three brothers*). That learner tosses the ball to another learner, who says something similar. The activity continues until all learners have spoken at least once about their family. Listen for use of *-s* with plural nouns. If necessary, do a separate review of the structure.
2. Show pictures of men and women to teach the words *man* and *woman*. Write the words on the board and have learners copy.

Presentation

1. Have learners turn to page 23 and look at the exercise at the top of the page. If necessary, use pictures to clarify the symbols for male and female. Have learners read the words for family members and indicate if they refer to a man or a woman. Check responses as a class.
2. Draw the male and female symbols on the board. Divide the class into two teams, and assign one gender to each team. One by one, team members must come up and write the word for a family member under the gender symbol assigned to that team.
3. Read lists of word pairs beginning with same letters *(name / number, desk / Davis, father / family, married / mother, husband / hello, parents / paper, sister / single, last / Lisa, book / board, welcome / wife)*. Stress the sound of the first letter in the words. Ask learners to name the letter that begins the words in each pair and say

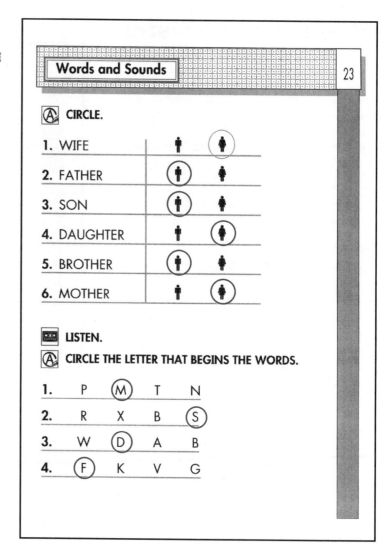

the sound that the letter makes. Repeat the sound for each pair, and have learners repeat.
4. ▄▄▄ Play the audiotape. Have learners complete the second exercise. Review answers as a class.

Expansion/Extension

- Have learners write the alphabet on a piece of paper. In pairs, have them go through the alphabet and check off the letters for which they are confident they know the sounds, and circle the letters they need to study more.

- Pairs of learners can look through Student Book lessons studied to date and write all the vocabulary words that start with the various letters. When they find more than one word for a letter, they can write all the examples found.

About Me

Purpose: To give practice in describing one-self and one's family

Teacher Preparation and Materials

1. A picture of your family or a picture of a family from a magazine

2. A stick-figure representation of Susan's family or a picture of a family from a magazine, with each member drawn on a separate card or piece of paper, or cut out separately and glued to a large index card

Warm-up

1. Review terms for family members: *mother, father, daughter, son.* Show learners the picture of your family or a family picture from a magazine. Point to the mother in the picture and say *This is _____. She is the mother.* Do the same for the other family members.

2. Present pictures of the four members of Susan Davis's family. Holding all four pictures, say *We are the Davis family.* Hold up the picture of the father and say *My name is Jim. I am the father.* Repeat for each family member (*My name is Susan. I am the mother. My name is Lisa. I am the daughter. My name is Nick. I am the son.*) Say the story again, and have learners say it with you. Then hold up individual pictures and ask *What is his/her name?* and *Who is he/she?* Clarify possessive pronouns as needed.

3. Review having learners say and write the name of their native country.

Presentation

1. Assign learners to groups of four to create "families." Have each group decide on a name for their family and each learner assume a role in the family. Have each family approach another one and introduce themselves, using the pattern from the *Warm-up* as a model.

2. Have each learner complete the exercise on page 24. When they have finished, have volunteers come to the front of the class individually and introduce themselves, using the information they have written in the exercise.

---

24 | **About Me**

A⃝ WRITE YOUR STORY.   Answers will vary.

MY NAME IS _____.

MY FIRST NAME IS _____.

MY LAST NAME IS _____.

I AM FROM _____.

I AM _____.

I HAVE _____ CHILD

I HAVE _____ BROTHER

I HAVE _____ SISTER

Expansion/Extension

- Review the concept of a family tree using your own family or Alex's or Susan's family as an example. Have learners create family trees showing their own families. Provide words for family members not yet taught, if necessary (*grandfather, grandmother, aunt, uncle,* etc.). Learners can label the family members with their names if they wish to do so.

- Have learners prepare a card or piece of paper listing the members of their immediate family and the relationship of each person to the learner. Encourage them to keep this list as reference when they need to fill out forms (FOR EXAMPLE: a family medical history).

123456 Summary
In the Neighborhood

Objectives

Functions
- Identifying and naming places in the neighborhood
- Identifying and interpreting signs in the neighborhood
- Using numbers for addresses and telephone numbers

Life Tasks
- Identifying places in a neighborhood
- Identifying and producing addresses
- Identifying and producing lowercase letters of the alphabet
- Identifying and producing numbers 0–9
- Identifying and interpreting *Walk, Don't Walk, Stop, Do Not Enter, Bus Stop,* and *No Parking* signs
- Understanding and writing telephone numbers
- Using 911 emergency number

Structures
- *Alex lives at . . .*
- *My telephone number is . . .*
- *Help!*
- *Emergency!*

Culture
- Addresses in the United States
- Telephone numbers in the United States
- Emergency services in the United States
- Emergency telephone number (911)

Vocabulary

Key words:
address
apartments
avenue
bank
drugstore
emergency
help
fire station
hospital
neighborhood
police station
post office
road
school
sign
street
supermarket
telephone
telephone number

Related words:
accident
bus stop
closed
do not enter
don't walk
fire
house
no parking
open
robbery
stop
walk

In the Neighborhood

Purpose: To activate prior knowledge about places and objects in the neighborhood; to give practice in distinguishing lowercase letters from capital letters; to introduce possessive pronouns

Teacher Preparation and Materials

Pictures of a house, apartment building, and school

Warm-up

Hold up a picture of a school. Ask learners to identify what kind of building it is. Say the word *school,* and have learners repeat. Spell the word, and have learners write it. Hold up pictures of an apartment building and a house and repeat the process. Select a learner, show the picture of the house or apartment building, and say *Your house.* Show the picture of the school, and say *Your school.* Holding the two pictures close and then apart, ask the learner if the two are close or far away from each other. Ask each learner.

Presentation

1. Have learners look at the picture on page 25 and identify any places that they recognize in the picture. Write these words on the board, say them, and spell them for the learners.

2. Have learners copy words from the board and use them to label the places shown in the picture.

3. Have learners look at the page title. Ask if they recognize anything. Point to the title, and say *What do you think this is? Letters? Words?* Ask what they think is the same as (or different from) letters and words they have previously seen.

4. Point to the word *neighborhood* and pronounce it. Have learners repeat. Point to the school in the picture and say *school.* Point to the surrounding area and say *neighborhood.* Point to another building that learners have identified and give the word for it. Point again to the surrounding area and say *neighborhood.* Use the picture of the house or apartments from the *Warm-up.* Tape it to the board and draw some quick streets and buildings around

it. Choose a learner who said his or her home was far away from the school. Label the picture _____'s *house/apartment.* Tape the picture of the school to the board, at some distance from that of the house, and draw some quick streets and buildings around it. Label it *our school.* Indicate the neighborhoods for both.

Expansion/Extension

Introduce or review all possessive pronouns. To introduce, closely hold a book or similar object and say *My book.* Give the book to other members of the class to illustrate other possessive pronouns, especially *his* and *her.*

Alex Lives Here

Purpose: To introduce addresses; to introduce lowercase letters

Teacher Preparation and Materials

1. Pictures of house and apartment building
2. 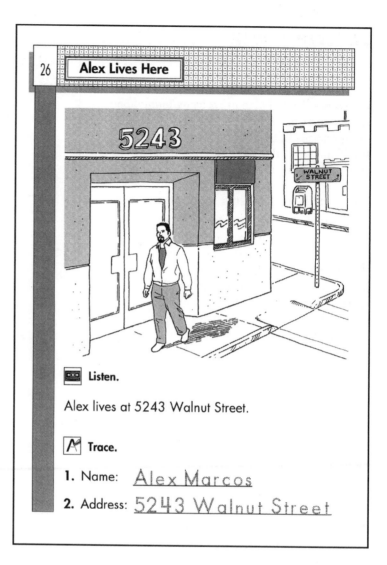 Audiotape for Literacy Level
3. Copies of Handouts 9 and 10, cut into game cards, enough sets so that teams of three to four people can each have a set *(Expansion/Extension)*

Warm-up

Show pictures and review words for house and apartment building. Ask learners *Where do you live?* If possible, elicit some addresses and write them on the board. If learners are not ready to say their address, proceed with activities in the Student Book.

Presentation

1. Ask learners to look at the picture on page 26 and identify who they see. Ask them to circle Alex's name on the page. Elicit as much description as possible. Ask *What else do you see?* Elicit what learners think is the connection between Alex and the building.
2. Play the audiotape. Ask *Where does Alex live?* Have learners read the sentence and say the street address.
3. Have learners trace the letters on both lines at the bottom of the Student Book page. Ask them to identify what they see there (numbers, letters). Ask what is different about the letters.
4. Introduce lowercase letters. Have learners find Alex Marcos's name in a previous unit and write it. Have a volunteer write the name on the board, using capital letters. Directly under it, write the name in capitals and lowercase letters. Have learners copy it. Ask if they think it's the same name.
5. Present the lowercase alphabet. First, write the capital letters of the alphabet in two vertical columns. Have learners copy them. Point to each letter and have learners name it. After they name a letter, write the lowercase letter beside it, point to it, and repeat the letter name. When

finished, have learners practice writing the lowercase letters next to the capital letters on their papers to create reference sheets for themselves.

Expansion/Extension

Divide the class into teams of three or four. Give each team a set of the game cards from Handouts 9 and 10. Mix the game cards, capitals and lowercase, and spread each set face down on a desk. Teams must attempt to match capitals and lowercase letters. The winning team is the one that makes the most successful matches.

Addresses

Purpose: To give practice in writing and saying addresses; to introduce use of capital and lowercase letters

Teacher Preparation and Materials

None

Warm-up

Have learners look at page 26, at the picture of Alex in front of his house. Ask them if they can match what they see in the sentence or the lines at the bottom of the page with anything in the picture. Ask them to guess what the word on the sign and the numbers mean.

Presentation

1. Have learners turn to page 27. Introduce addresses. Ask learners to look at the first picture and trace the numbers on the line. Ask learners to look at the address and indicate what addresses contain (numbers and words or names). Have them find the number in the picture. Ask what the number means.

2. Have learners write the remaining numbers for the addresses in items 2 and 3 of the exercise.

3. Have learners look at the picture and the address in item 4. Ask what the number is in the address. Then have learners trace the words. Have them find the words in the picture. Ask what the words represent.

4. Have learners write the street names for the remaining addresses in the exercise. Ask them to look at and say the last word in all the addresses. Point out that all the words *(avenue, street, road)* are different words for streets.

5. Write several of the street names on the board, along with the names of the two characters from previous units, Susan Davis and Alex Marcos. Ask learners where they find the "big" (capital) letters. Explain that those letters are used at beginning of names. Write your name on the board in all capital letters. Have learners rewrite using capitals and lowercase letters in the proper places. Have them write

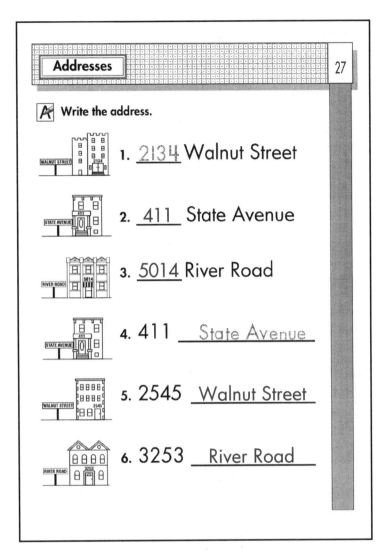

their own names with capitals and lowercase letters, then switch papers with a partner and review.

6. Have learners write their own names and addresses in capitals and lowercase letters on the inside cover of their Student Books.

Expansion/Extension

Have learners interview three people outside of class and record their names and street addresses. Have them report back to the class, and discuss any items that are new (FOR EXAMPLE: an apartment number or a new word for street).

Places in the Neighborhood

Purpose: To introduce words for common places in a neighborhood

Teacher Preparation and Materials

1. Items found in various places in a neighborhood (FOR EXAMPLE: stamps and letters for a post office, medications for a drugstore)

2. Copies of Handout 12, Neighborhood Places, using only the cards for bank, supermarket, post office, drugstore, and the related items; duplicate and cut so that there is one set for every two learners in the class *(Expansion/Extension)*

Warm-up

1. If possible, take learners for a walk in the area around the school. Ask them to identify buildings and places that they know. Ask them to keep notes or draw pictures so that they will remember what they saw.

2. Look at the picture on page 25. Have learners identify any buildings that they recognize.

Presentation

1. Write the words for various neighborhood places (FOR EXAMPLE: *supermarket, post office*) on the board in all lowercase letters. Say the words, and have learners repeat them. Have learners spell the words as you point to the letters.

2. Hold up items found in neighborhood places. Elicit or show learners where you go for each thing. Hold up each item, name it, say the word for the place where you find it, and have learners repeat the words. Then hold up each item, name it, and write the names on the board. Ask learners to identify which place each piece is from and then point to the name of the place on the board.

3. Have learners individually complete the exercise. When finished, check responses together as a class. Hold up the corresponding item for each place and have learners name it.

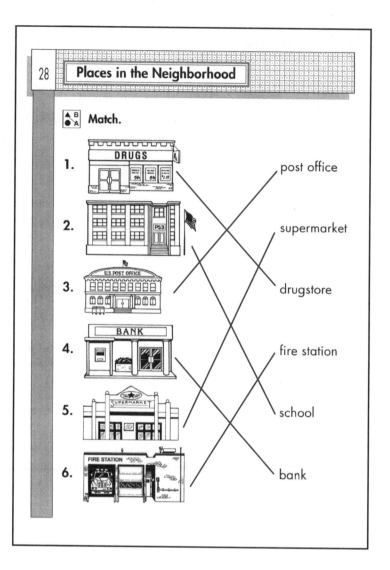

Expansion/Extension

- Have learners create a Language Experience Approach (LEA) story based on the neighborhood trip, their notes, and the vocabulary in this lesson. Write the story on the board. Have the learners read the story and copy it.

- Put learners in pairs. Distribute sets of cards from Handout 12 and have them play Concentration, matching places and items.

- Give learners a list of the places discussed. Ask them to record the specific names of these places in their neighborhood. Have them report their findings to the class and compare what they found.

Signs in the Neighborhood

Purpose: To introduce and give practice in recognizing common street signs

Teacher Preparation and Materials

1. Examples of several signs common in the school (FOR EXAMPLE: *Office, Exit,* man/woman bathroom symbols) drawn on chart paper

2. Flash cards with one sign from this lesson on each (two sets)

3. Handout 11, Neighborhood Signs *(Expansion/Extension)*

Warm-up

Show examples drawn on chart paper (or on the board) of several simple, common signs found in the school. Ask learners to go out and find these signs and then report to the class where they found them. Discuss what they mean. Add drawings of any additional signs learners found and want to discuss.

Presentation

1. Have learners turn to page 29 and look at the signs at the top of the page. Use gestures, head movements, or *OK* and *Not OK* to demonstrate that one is a *yes* sign, telling that something is allowed, and the other is a *no* sign, stopping an action.

2. Have learners look at the picture at the bottom of the page. Ask them to circle all the signs that they see in the picture. Point to each sign and read the lettering on the sign. Have the learners repeat. Ask the learners to guess what each sign means. Confirm or correct learners' guesses by either doing a simple drawing on the board or acting out the meaning. For example, for *Do Not Enter,* draw the sign on the board and pretend to start to make a turn. Point to the sign on the board, and pretend to back up the car and go another way.

3. Have learners categorize the signs in the bottom picture as *yes* or *no* signs. (It may help to associate the *no* signs with the symbol of a circle with a diagonal line through it.)

4. Show flash cards of signs, and have volunteers read or explain them.

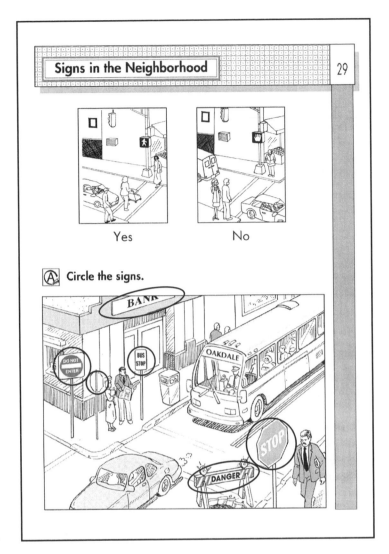

Expansion/Extension

- Divide the learners into two teams, and give each team a set of flash cards with signs on them. Have the first member of each team draw a card and act out the sign shown. Team members guess what it says. The first team to complete their stack wins. (The game can be played with learners drawing clues about the signs, rather than acting them out.)

- Ask learners to use Handout 11 to record the signs that they see in their neighborhoods. They can also draw examples of signs not listed on the back of the sheet. Have learners compare their findings, guess what any new signs mean, and discuss which signs seem to be the most common.

Police, Fire, and Hospital

Purpose: To introduce words for emergency services

Teacher Preparation and Materials

1. Copies of Handout 12, Neighborhood Places (using all pieces) (enough sets for every two people in the class)
2. Pictures of a robbery and a building on fire

Warm-up

1. Put a list of the neighborhood places learned so far on the board. Ask learners to say each one. Show a picture of a robbery. Ask learners if they would go to the supermarket for help in this situation. (No) Ask what they go to the supermarket for. Repeat this process for each place listed.
2. Ask where they would go for help in case of a robbery like the one in the picture. If a learner can say *police*, write the word on the board and have all learners say the word and copy it. Then show the picture of the building on fire. Ask where they would get help in that situation. Try to elicit *fireman* or a related word. Similarly, write the word on the board for learners to say and copy.

Presentation

1. Have learners turn to page 30 and look at the pictures at the top of the page. Pronounce the name of the first place; have learners repeat. Write the name on the board in lowercase letters. Have learners copy, labeling the picture in the book. Repeat the process for the other two places, then repeat for the emergencies. Have learners match the emergencies to the places that would handle them.
2. Pair learners and give each pair a set of cards from Handout 12. Have them play Concentration, matching places, including emergency services, with associated scenes or items.
3. Have learners complete the second exercise on the page, writing the separate

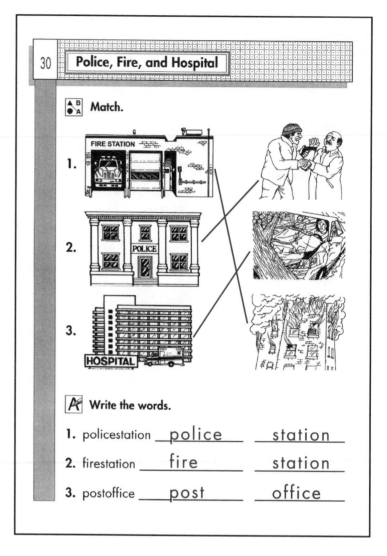

words. Then have learners categorize other neighborhood place names as having one or two words.

Expansion/Extension

- Ask learners to illustrate, act out, or describe other types of emergencies that might be encountered. As a class, discuss which emergency service would handle it. (Supply words for other services, like *poison control* or *landlord*, if learners raise an issue that would be better served by one of those services.)

- Invite a member of the police or fire department to visit the class to talk to the learners. This visit would serve simply to familiarize learners generally with the service agencies. If the visitor wants to make a presentation, ask for an outline or simplified print materials produced by the emergency service so that you can preteach vocabulary and concepts to prepare learners before the visit.

Emergency!

Purpose: To introduce the 911 emergency number; to introduce and give practice with numbers 6–9

Teacher Preparation and Materials

1. Pictures of various accidents or emergencies (FOR EXAMPLE: fire, robbery, car accident, person having heart attack)
2. A real or toy telephone
3. A large drawing of a telephone keypad, on chart paper or the board

Warm-up

Show various pictures of emergencies or accidents. Ask learners what is happening and what they would do in each situation. Write on the board *Police, Fire,* and *Hospital.* For each picture, ask learners which service they would use, and tape the picture under the appropriate word.

Presentation

1. Have learners turn to page 31 and look at the picture at the top of the page. Ask *What is happening? What is the person doing? What do you think the person is saying?* Read the words for the learners. Have them repeat.

2. Present 911 as the emergency number. Hold up the emergency/accident pictures used in the *Warm-up* and say for each, *What do you do? Call 911.* Demonstrate on the telephone, saying the numbers as you press them. (If you have a large class, also demonstrate on the enlarged drawing of the telephone keypad so learners can see more easily.) Have learners demonstrate dialing 911 individually, using the telephone or the keypad on the Student Book page.

3. Have learners look at the enlarged telephone keypad and at the keypad on the pages. Point to the number 1 and ask what number it is. Do the same for numbers 2 to 5, which they already know. Point to numbers 6 through 9, and ask first if any learners know the numbers. If not, point to each, say the number, and have learners repeat. Point to 0 and ask them to identify it.

4. Have learners individually practice tracing and writing the numbers on the lower half of the Student Book page.

Expansion/Extension

Model a simplified 911 call. Show picture of a fire. Dial 911 on the phone and say *Help. Emergency. A fire.* In pairs, have learners practice following that model for all the emergency pictures. Once learners feel comfortable saying this, help them add their address to the call and practice again.

On the Phone

Purpose: To introduce and give practice in writing and saying telephone numbers

Teacher Preparation and Materials

1. ▦ Audiotape for Literacy Level
2. Copy of the white pages phone book *(Expansion/Extension)*

Warm-up

Dictate groups of five numbers for the learners to write on a piece of paper. Do three to five groups. Have pairs of learners compare papers to review their answers.

Presentation

1. Have learners look at the picture at the top of page 32. Ask *What is this?* Point to the word *telephone,* and say it. Have learners repeat. Spell the word, and have learners write it. Have them look at the next picture and words. Ask *What is the person using? What are the two words?* Have learners point to and identify the words *telephone* and *number.* Then ask what they see below the words.

2. Introduce telephone numbers. Write a telephone number on the board in the usual way ((000) 000-0000); use an area code common for your area.) Read the telephone number, orally grouping the digits as native speakers do (first three numbers, next three, final four). Have learners repeat. Write several more numbers on the board and call on volunteers to say them.

3. Write your telephone number (or make one up) and say it. Identify it as your telephone number. Say *My telephone number is . . .* Have learners repeat the whole sentence. Have them write their telephone numbers on the lines in the Student Book. Circulate, and have learners tell you their telephone numbers. (Do this privately, as some learners may not be comfortable giving their telephone numbers to the whole class.) **Note:** If you live in an area where an area code is not needed for a local call, be sure learners understand this.

4. ▦ Have learners listen to the audiotape and complete the second exercise. Review the correct answers as a class. ▦ Have

learners listen again, and write the correct numbers for the items where they answered no.

Expansion/Extension

Introduce the white pages telephone book as a way to find personal telephone numbers. Have learners browse through the book. Encourage learners to look up their own phone number, if they are listed, or the phone number of someone they know. Point out where they can find white pages business listings, listings for government offices, and emergency service numbers.

My Telephone Number

Purpose: To give practice in listening for and giving telephone numbers

Teacher Preparation and Materials
■■■ Audiotape for Literacy Level

Warm-up
Dictate several telephone numbers, and have learners write them. Have volunteers write the numbers on the board for learners to check their work.

Presentation
1. Have learners turn to page 33. ■■■ Play the audiotape. Have learners listen for the first section of information on Alex Marcos. Have them trace the letters and numbers. Ask learners *What is his name?* (Alex Marcos) *What is his telephone number?* (713-691-8836).

2. ■■■ Have learners listen to the audiotape for the next section and then fill in the words and numbers that are missing. ■■■ Repeat the audio as necessary. Ask what the woman's name is. (Susan Davis) Ask what her telephone number is. (713-886-5192)

3. Have learners fill in their own information in the bottom section.

4. Ask learners to point out "big" (capital) letters on the Student Book page. Ask where they are. Explain that capital letters are also used to start sentences. Write an example of a letter, a name, and a sentence on the board. Show that letters can be capital and that names and sentences begin with capital letters. Write several more names and sentences from previous lessons, and have learners indicate where capital letters are needed.

5. Model a conversation in which one person is asking for someone's telephone number. Person one says "What is your telephone number?" Person two responds with the telephone number. Person one writes down the number and then repeats the number with question intonation to confirm. Person two either confirms or corrects. Have learners chorally repeat the

whole conversation. Pair learners, and have them say the conversation themselves.

Expansion/Extension

Ask learners to write their name and a telephone number on a piece of paper. (They could make up a number, if they prefer.) Ask learners to choose a partner and read their information to the partner. The partner records the information, asking for spelling of name or confirmation of number as necessary. Have learners exchange roles. Then have each check what the other wrote.

My Personal Information

Purpose: To give learners the chance to record personal information and important telephone numbers for reference

Teacher Preparation and Materials

1. A copy of the local telephone white pages
2. Copies of the emergency numbers page from the telephone book (one copy for every two learners in the class)

Warm-up

1. Have learners review saying and writing their address and telephone number. Ask *What number do you call in an emergency?* Elicit *911*.
2. Write *fire station, police station,* and *hospital* on the board. Point to each, and have learners read the words. Discuss when you would call each one. Ask learners for the telephone numbers for each. If they say 911, agree, saying that number is for emergencies. Explain that there are other numbers to use if it's not an emergency

Presentation

1. Have learners turn to page 34 and complete the first section of the form individually. In the second section, for the emergency number, have the class chorally respond with the 911 number, and have each learner write the number on the page.
2. Pair learners, and give each pair a copy of the emergency numbers page from the telephone book. Ask them to find the words *police, fire,* and *hospital* on the page and circle the section that deals with these organizations. Remind learners that, in addition to 911, police stations, fire stations, and hospitals also have regular telephone numbers. Depending on the local telephone book, have learners find the regular numbers on the emergency numbers page or guide them to the appropriate section of a full phone book. Have learners copy the numbers onto the appropriate lines. If hospitals are not listed on the emergency page, find numbers and addresses for a few local hospitals and help learners determine which is closest to

their homes. Advise learners to make a copy of this page and keep the sheet close to their telephone at home.

Expansion/Extension

- Have learners copy and modify the form on the Student Book page so that it would be useful for roommates, housemates, or relatives who may not read English. They can add drawings or key words in their native languages or anything else they think might help others also use the reference. Encourage learners to give their modified version to friends or relatives who can use it.

- Have learners practice saying the personal information on this page aloud (privately to you if they prefer) so they can speak confidently if they have to give the information to any emergency service that they call.

---

34 | **My Personal Information**

A+ **Write.** Answers will vary.

Information

Personal Information

Name_____

Address_____

_____

Telephone Number_____

Emergency Information

Emergency Number_____

Fire_____

Police_____

Hospital_____

123456 Summary
Going Shopping

Objectives

Functions
- Identifying and naming days of the week
- Talking about money and writing monetary amounts
- Identifying, saying, and writing numbers 10–49
- Identifying and naming items of food

Life Tasks
- Talking about days of the week and weekly schedules
- Dealing with money and prices
- Shopping for food

Structures
- Questions with *when? where?* and *how much?*

Culture
- Shopping for food in the United States
- Money in the United States

Vocabulary

Key words:

bread
carrot
cent
chicken
dollar
egg
food
Friday
grape
milk
Monday
money
Saturday
Sunday
Thursday
to shop
Tuesday
Wednesday
when
where

Related words:

bill
cash
cashier
check out
coin
dime
nickel
penny
quarter
receipt

Going Shopping

Purpose: To introduce words for some common activities

Teacher Preparation and Materials

1. Pictures from magazines or other sources showing common activities: eating, working, watching TV, sleeping, or others like these

2. Photocopies of the action pictures, at least one for every learner (If two pictures can be copied on a page or if each learner can have pictures of more than one activity, that is even better.)

Warm-up

Have learners turn to page 35 and look at the picture on the page. Ask *Where is the woman? What is she doing?* Write any words the learners produce on the board. Say the words, and have learners repeat. Have learners label the picture with the words that they produced.

Presentation

1. Point to the words at the top of the page. Say them, and have learners repeat. Draw a stick figure on the board or chart paper representing the woman in the picture on page 35. Draw a large speech bubble coming from the woman's mouth. Write *I shop* in the speech bubble, and show it so that the class can see it. Point to the woman, and say *I shop.* Repeat, and have learners repeat. Have learners draw the same speech bubble and sentence on their Student Book pages. Make sure learners understand the word *shop.* Act it out or elicit explanations from learners if necessary.

2. Show learners pictures of other activities. For each, say the name of the activity and write it on the board (FOR EXAMPLE: *eat, work, watch TV, sleep*). Repeat each word, and have learners repeat it. Then go back and change the first activity into a sentence with *I.* Say the sentence, and have learners repeat. Call on volunteers to change the other action words into sentences.

3. Give learners copies of the pictures, and have them draw on speech bubbles and write the appropriate sentence in the bubble.

Expansion/Extension

Ask learners to act out other things that they do during the day, and write the words on the board for them. Say each one, and have learners repeat. Have learners turn each into a sentence with *I.* Have learners say each sentence. Have them choose a sentence and illustrate it. Say each sentence, and have learners raise their hands if they do it.

Going Shopping: When?

Purpose: To introduce the days of the week; to give practice in responding to questions with *when*

Teacher Preparation and Materials

1. Calendar for a week or a month, showing days of the week
2. ▆▆▆ Audiotape for Literacy Level

Warm-up

1. Show learners the calendar. Point to the current day. Say *Today is . . .* (current day of the week). Elicit any days of the week that learners can say. Prompt with *Today is . . . ? Yesterday? Tomorrow?* If learners can say any of the days of the week, write the day on the board, say it, and have the whole class repeat.

2. Have learners turn to page 36 and look at the picture at the top of the page. Ask *What's happening? Where is the woman going? What is she going to do? Do you do this?* Write any words the learners produce on the board. This should produce at least *woman, shop,* and *supermarket.*

Presentation

1. ▆▆▆ Play the audiotape for the learners and have them follow along with the sentences on the Student Book page. Chorally repeat the sentences without the tape and have them fill in the blank. If necessary, spell the missing part of the word while learners write.

2. Ask the question *When?* Exaggerate the rising voice at the end to show clearly that it's a question. Have learners repeat. Ask *When does she shop?* (Saturday)

3. Point to the days of the week on the calendar at the bottom of the page. Say each day, and have the learners repeat after you. Ask the learners what these words are. Elicit the word *days* (point to the individual days); if possible, explain that they are days of the week (indicate the week). Pointing to the picture and the words above, say *I shop on Saturday.* Ask learners to circle the day on the calendar on which the woman shops.

Expansion/Extension

Point to the dialogue at the top of the page. Say *I shop.* Signal to the learners that they should say, together, *When?* Then say *I shop on Wednesday.* Point to a learner, and indicate that the learner should say *I shop.* Again, elicit the question *When?* and learner replies, filling in with the name of a day. Continue around the class until all learners have participated in the dialogue.

Days of the Week

Purpose: To give practice in saying and writing the days of the week

Teacher Preparation and Materials

1. Set of cards with a day of the week written on each card
2. ▇▇▇ Audiotape for Literacy Level
3. Beachball, beanbag, or other object that can be tossed

Warm-up

Have learners look at the calendar on page 36. Point to the days of the week across the top and ask what they are. Say each day, and have learners repeat. Ask *What is the same in each word? (-day)* Have learners circle that part.

Presentation

1. Have learners turn to page 37 and trace or write the missing letters to complete the names of the days of the week at the top of the page. When finished, say all the days again, have learners repeat, and ask volunteers to spell the individual days while the rest of the class checks the work.

2. Write *Today* on the board. Ask learners to identify the day of the week it is. Write *Tomorrow* and *Yesterday* and do the same.

3. Have seven volunteers come forward. Give them each a card with a day of the week on it. Have them stand, randomly sequenced, in front of the class. Ask the class to call out the name of the day that should be first. Move the learner to the first position in a line. Repeat until the days are in order.

4. Hold the ball or other object to be tossed. Call out the name of a day of the week and then toss the ball to a learner. The learner must call out the name of the next day. That learner then tosses the ball to another, who must name the next day. Continue until all learners have named a day.

5. Have learners look at the pictures at the bottom of the page. Ask them what is happening in each. Write the action words for each picture: *work* and *go to school.* Say

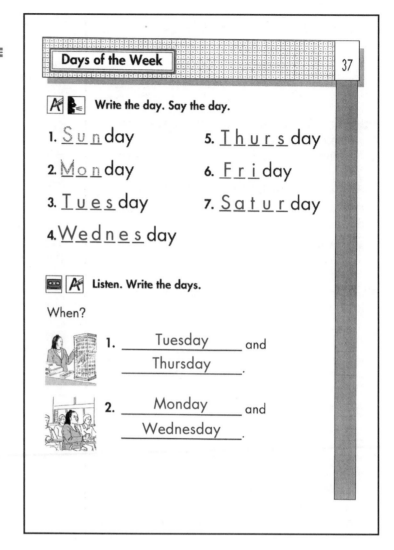

the words, and have learners repeat. Say them again, this time in the sentence *I work/go to school.* Point to the days of the week written there and say, *I shop. When? Sunday? Monday?* (and so on) ▇▇▇ Have learners listen to the audiotape and complete the exercise.

Expansion/Extension

Post cards with days on them around the room. Write *I work, I shop,* and *I go to school* on the board. Have learners brainstorm other actions, and write them. Say each sentence and ask, *When?* As you do, have learners go and stand by the day on which they do that action. Later, have learners record their answers on paper in sentence form (FOR EXAMPLE: I go to school on Monday, Wednesday, and Friday.)

Numbers 10–49

Purpose: To review numbers 0–9; to give practice in saying and writing numbers 10–49

Teacher Preparation and Materials

1. Two different randomly sequenced lists of numbers 10–19 (copies of one list for half the class; copies of the other for the other half)
2. Copies of Handout 13, My Calendar (one copy per learner) *(Expansion/Extension)*

Warm-up

1. Have learners stand in a circle and count off from 0 to 9. When they reach 9, have the next person start again with 0. If necessary, repeat the sequence until all learners have said a number.
2. Have learners count off again, but this time have them reverse the sequence, counting from 9 to 0.

Presentation

1. Write the numbers 0–9 on the board, and have the class say them together. Then have learners turn to page 38 and look at the first column of numbers. Write the numbers on the board, starting with 10. Say each number as you write it, and have learners repeat. Stop at 19. Repeat numbers 10–19 as learners write each number next to the one in their books.
2. Randomly write numbers between 0 and 19 on the board, and have learners call out the number after you write it.
3. Pair learners. Give each member of the pair a different list of numbers 10–19. The first learner reads the numbers on his list, the second learner writes them, and they compare the written work to the list. Then have learners switch roles and repeat the process.
4. Have learners look at the second column. Point to the number 20, and say it. Have learners repeat. Continue down the column, with learners repeating. Say numbers 20–29 again, as learners write each number next to the one in their books.
5. Start the next column the same way. When you say 32, have learners trace the 2. For

the rest of the column, say *thirty* . . . , and have learners call out the second numeral and write it. For the last column, introduce the number 40, but have volunteers say the complete numbers after that. Have learners repeat each number after it is given and write it in their books.

Expansion/Extension

Give learners copies of Handout 13 and have them create their own calendars for the current month, filling in the days and numbers for the dates. Have learners write various activities (FOR EXAMPLE: I work, I shop) on the days that they do them.

---

38 | **Numbers 10–49**

Ⓜ Ⓐ Trace. Write.

10 _10_	20 _20_	30 _0_	40 _0_
11 _11_	21 _21_	3 _1_	4 _1_
12 _12_	22 _22_	32 _2_	42 _2_
13 _13_	23 _23_	33 _3_	43 _3_
14 _14_	24 _24_	34 _4_	44 _44_
15 _15_	25 _25_	35 _35_	45 _45_
16 _16_	26 _26_	36 _36_	46 _46_
17 _17_	27 _27_	37 _37_	47 _47_
18 _18_	28 _28_	38 _38_	48 _48_
19 _19_	29 _29_	39 _39_	49 _49_

Going Shopping: Where?

Purpose: To give practice in responding to questions with *where*

Teacher Preparation and Materials

1. Pictures of places for which learners know sight words: supermarket, drugstore, post office, fire station, school
2. ▦ Audiotape for Literacy Level
3. Pictures of various items that can be purchased at a supermarket, post office, or drugstore

Warm-up

1. Have learners turn to page 36 and look again at the picture at the top of the page. Review the sentence *I shop on Saturday.* Point to the picture and ask *When?* Elicit the answer, and write *I shop on Saturday* on the board.
2. Review words for places in a neighborhood. Hold up pictures, ask *Where?* and elicit the words. Write or have volunteers write each place word on the board.

Presentation

1. Have learners turn to page 39 and look at the picture at the top and the words next to it. Ask them to say and underline words they recognize. Point to the word *Where.* Write *when* and *where* on the board. Show that they are different words. Have a volunteer come up and underline or circle the letters that are different.
2. ▦ Play the audiotape, and have learners follow along on the Student Book page. Have learners repeat the sentences chorally without the tape and then fill in the blank.
3. Ask the question *Where?* stressing the rising intonation to signal a question. Repeat, pointing to the question mark. Ask *Where does she shop?* Elicit the answer "At the supermarket."
4. Write some names of supermarkets in the area on the board. Point to each, and say it. Have learners repeat. Ask learners what they are. Write *supermarket* at the top of the list. Say *I shop at the supermarket. I shop at . . .* (give the name of a

specific supermarket). Ask learners individually *Where do you shop?* Prompt as necessary to have learners answer "I shop at . . . ," giving the name of the specific supermarkets.
5. Have learners look the exercise at the bottom of the page. Point to the first picture and ask *Where do you shop?* Have learners circle the word and say it. Point to the next picture and repeat.
6. Show pictures of various items that can be purchased at the supermarket, drugstore, or post office. For each picture, ask *Where do you shop?* Call on a learner to respond. If there is more than one place, probe for all.

Expansion/Extension

Have learners interview people outside class to find out where they shop, getting names of specific stores.

Shopping for Food

Purpose: To introduce and give practice with food vocabulary

Teacher Preparation and Materials

1. Blank paper (one sheet per learner)

2. Copies of Handout 15, Food, cut into cards, one set per learner; if possible, one set enlarged as well

3. Circulars from local supermarkets (at least one per learner)
   (Expansion/Extension)

Warm-up

Give learners each a sheet of paper, and have them draw a picture of a supermarket in the center. Around it, have learners draw pictures of things they find there. If necessary, first model the picture of the supermarket and one or two items around it on the board. Have learners show their pictures and name any items for which they know the word in English. Encourage other learners to give the words for items they know.

Presentation

1. Have learners turn to page 40 and look at the picture at the top. Ask *I shop . . . when?* and have them answer. Repeat with *I shop . . . where?* Point to the Student Book page and say *I shop . . . for what? I shop for food.* Read the sentence together. Elicit or give an explanation of *food.* Ask learners what the person is holding. Write *shopping list* on the board, and have learners label it in their books.

2. Ask if learners can use the pictures to identify any items on the list. Refer to items by number if any learners say the words. Then read all the items on the list, and have learners repeat. Ask if learners can match any word from the list to a picture in the exercise. Refer to items by number to clarify any matches that learners suggest. Then point to the chicken on the list and say *chicken,* point to the picture of chicken in the exercise, and have learners copy the word under the picture. Repeat until all pictures are labeled.

3. Give each learner a set of the food cards from Handout 15. Name a food, and have learners select the card from the set. Do

this first for the foods on page 40. Then introduce the foods on the remaining cards. Say words for foods at random until all cards have been identified.

Expansion/Extension

- Have learners choose food items from the food cards and create a grocery list like the one in the Student Book. Then pair learners. Have one learner read his or her list while the second learner finds the cards for the items read and gives them to the first learner. The first learner checks to be sure the list and the cards match. Then have learners switch roles.

- Give learners circulars from local supermarkets, and have them circle pictures and words for items covered in the lesson.

How Much?

Purpose: To give practice in identifying money; to give practice in identifying, saying, and writing different amounts of money

Teacher Preparation and Materials

1. 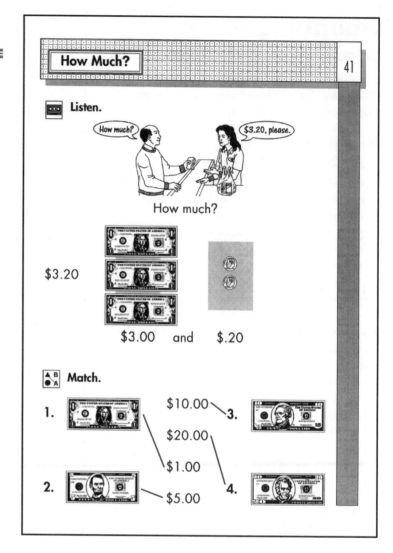 Audiotape for Literacy Level
2. Real or play money, including one each of the $1, $5, $10, and $20 bills and enough bills and coins for $3.20
3. Multiple copies of Handout 14, Money (bills only, cut out, enough that each learner has at least several copies of each bill) *(Expansion/Extension)*

Warm-up

Show a variety of bills and coins. Ask learners to identify what they see. Hold up the bills, and say *dollars.* Have learners repeat. Repeat with the coins, and say *cents.* Ask learners to look at the bills and say the numbers that they see on them.

Presentation

1. Have learners turn to page 41 and look at the picture at the top. Ask *What is happening? Where are the people? What are they doing?* Ask learners what they think the people are saying.

2. Play the audiotape. Have learners listen and follow the conversation in the picture. Repeat the conversation chorally with learners. Say the question, and have learners point to the person saying it. Then say the answer, and have learners point to the person saying it.

3. Have learners look at the question and the money under the picture. Say *How much? Three dollars and twenty cents,* holding up three $1 bills and two dimes. Show learners that the bills and coins are equivalent to the money pictured on the page. Count out the money to show how the bills and coins make $3.20, and have learners say the amounts with you.

4. Have learners look at the bills pictured in the exercise. Ask them to look at the number on the first one. Say *one dollar.* Have learners repeat. Write $1.00 on the board, say it, and have learners write and say it. Repeat with the other three bills.

5. Hold up examples of bills, and have learners call out the amount they represent (one dollar, five dollars, etc.).

6. Have learners complete the matching exercise.

Expansion/Extension

- Give learners sets of the bills from Handout 14. Write a dollar amount on the board (FOR EXAMPLE: $7.00, $23.00), and demonstrate putting bills together to equal that amount. Write another figure, and have learners do it with you. Write several amounts on the board, and have learners put together the bills to equal each one. Check by having learners count out the bills they put together for each amount.

- Have learners write amounts of money (dollars only) and quiz each other on putting together bills to equal the amounts.

Money

Purpose: To give practice in identifying money; to give practice in identifying, saying, and writing amounts of money

Teacher Preparation and Materials

1. Real or play money, including one each of the $1, $5, $10, and $20 bills and one penny, nickel, dime, and quarter

2. Multiple copies of Handout 14, Money (cut out, enough that each learner has at least several copies of each bill and coin)

3. Extra coins (real or from Handout 14, one set for every two learners)

Warm-up

1. Hold up individual bills, and have learners identify them. Combine bills, and have learners identify the amounts.

2. Hold up individual coins, review the word *cents,* and ask if learners can identify the amounts represented.

3. Put learners in pairs, and give each pair a set of real coins or coins from Handout 14. Hold up a penny and say *one cent.* Have learners repeat. Write $.01 on the board and say *one cent* again. Have learners repeat and copy. Repeat for each coin. Point to amounts on the board randomly, and have learners say each amount, holding up the appropriate coin as they do so.

Presentation

1. Have learners turn to page 42 and complete the matching exercise at the top of the page.

2. Write $.35 on the board, and ask learners to say it. Model and have them repeat if they are not able to read the amount easily. Show a quarter, and say *25 cents.* Repeat with a dime. Combine the coins and say *35 cents.* Have pairs combine the same coins and also say the amount. Write several other prices on the board (FOR EXAMPLE: $.11, $.15, $.38). Have learners say the amounts. Then have pairs combine coins to show the amounts.

3. Write $3.20 on the board and have learners say it. Ask them to identify the dollars and underline the 3. Ask them to identify the cents and underline the 20. Write sev-

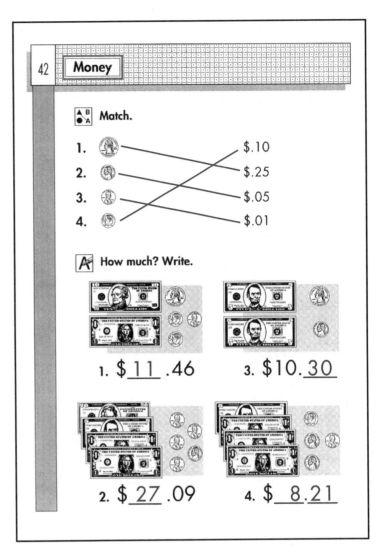

eral other prices on the board, and repeat the process. Give pairs of learners sets of the money from Handout 14. Have pairs combine their bills and coins to equal the amounts written on the board. Circulate to check the combinations.

4. Have learners look at the picture in the first item in the second exercise. Have learners count the bills and write the amount in the blank. Have them count the coins and check against the number on the page. Have learners complete the exercise individually and compare answers with their partners.

Expansion/Extension

Introduce other names for coins: *quarter, dime, nickel, penny.* Have learners find *quarter* and *dime* on the real coins.

Paying for Food

Purpose: To give practice in identifying amounts of money

Teacher Preparation and Materials

1. Copies of a simple receipt from a supermarket or drugstore
2. Sets of money (bills and coins) from Handout 14, Money
3. 📼 Audiotape for Literacy Level
4. Multiple copies of circulars from several local supermarkets (*Expansion/Extension*)

Warm-up

1. Say five prices, and have learners write the prices they hear. Have volunteers write each price on the board, and have learners check their answers.

2. Give learners copies of a simple receipt from a local supermarket or drugstore. Hold up a copy or the original receipt, and say *receipt*. Have learners repeat. Ask learners where they get a receipt. Have volunteers read the price of each item on the receipt. Write the prices on the board as they say them. Ask *What is the total?* Write *total* on the board. Have learners find the word on the bill. Ask *What does* total *mean?* and elicit an explanation. Ask learners for the amount of the total. Draw a line under the prices on the board and write the total beneath it. Give the learners each a set of the money from Handout 14. Have them combine bills and coins to pay the amount on the receipt. Circulate and check that they are correct.

Presentation

1. Have learners turn to page 43 and look at the first exercise. Ask them what they see (a receipt). Have volunteers read the items and their prices on the receipt. Ask for the total. Have learners circle the set of money in the pictures to the right that matches the total.

2. Have learners use the money from Handout 14 to create other combinations of bills and coins to pay the amount.

3. 📼 Play the audiotape, and have learners complete the exercise at the bottom of the page. Review the answers as a class. Prac-

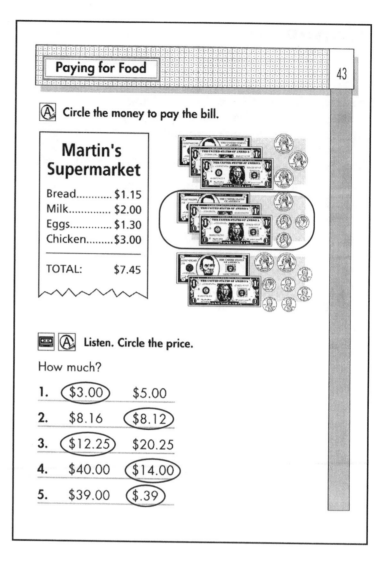

tice saying and listening for any numbers that learners identify as difficult to distinguish, such as $14.00 and $40.00 or $39.00 and $.39. Practice distinguishing other similar numbers (FOR EXAMPLE: 13 and 30).

Expansion/Extension

- Bring in circulars from competing supermarkets in the area. Pair learners. Have them find the same food items in the different circulars and compare the prices. Have each pair record at least three items and their prices and report back to the class where the best price can be found.

- Have learners prepare a simple shopping list. Then have them choose one of the supermarkets and use its circular to find prices for as many of the items on their lists as possible.

I Shop on Friday

Purpose: To give practice in reading and writing about shopping

Teacher Preparation and Materials

1. Pictures of vocabulary items: supermarket, chicken, bread, milk
2. Pictures of a supermarket customer and a checkout clerk
3. Calendar showing days of the week
4. ▣▣▣ Audiotape for Literacy Level
5. Cards or sheets of paper with question words *When? Where? What?* and *How much?*

Warm-up

1. Review key vocabulary for the story on page 44. Show pictures, and have learners say the words. Ask *Who is he/she? What is she doing? Where is he?*
2. Review days of the week using a calendar.

Presentation

1. Have learners turn to page 44. Have them look at the pictures with the story, name items that they know, and describe what they think is happening.
2. ▣▣▣ Play the audiotape, and have learners follow the story in their books. Then read the story aloud, and have learners read along with you.
3. Review the details in the story orally. Say *I shop . . . When?* Prompt learners to respond "On Friday." Say *I shop . . . Where?* and elicit "At the supermarket." Continue the pattern with *What?* and *How much?*
4. Ask the learners to read the words at the bottom of the page aloud. Repeat each to be sure learners are using question intonation. Ask *When?* Have learners individually underline the answer to the question in the story, then call out the answer. Have them write the answer in the Student Book. Repeat the process for items 2 and 3. Circulate to check that answers have been copied correctly.
5. Hold up cards showing question words *When? Where? What?* and *How much?* at random. Have learners respond appropriately with details from the story.

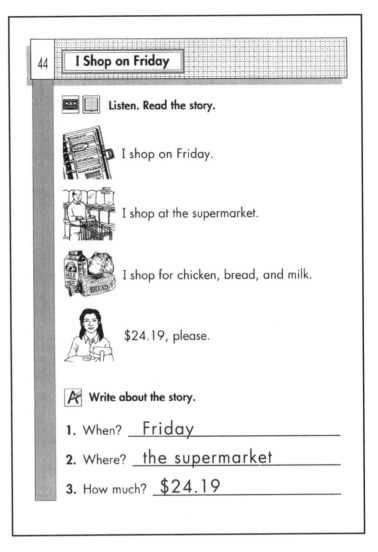

Expansion/Extension

- Print the story on the board or on a piece of chart paper. Underline *Friday, supermarket, chicken, bread, milk,* and *$24.19.* Have learners copy the story, inserting their own information for the underlined items. Have volunteers read their new stories to the class.

- Hold up cards with question words. Have learners answer with their own information or with details of a new version of the story that has just been read to them.

I Am Sick

Objectives

Functions

- Identifying and naming body parts
- Identifying and naming symptoms or illnesses
- Expressing times of day

Life Tasks

- Identifying body parts
- Calling a doctor's office and making an appointment
- Describing symptoms and health problems
- Telling time; recognizing times of day

Structures

- *I am sick.*
- *My . . . hurts.*
- *I have a . . .*
- *What's wrong?*
- *Can you come at . . . ?*

Culture

- Making appointments
- Going to the doctor in the United States

Vocabulary

Key words:

arm
back
chest
cough
doctor
ear
eye
fever
foot
hand
head
hour
hurt
leg
minute
nose
office
runny nose
sick
stomach
throat
time

Related words:

body
clock
conversation
hands (of a clock)
nurse
o'clock
pain
receptionist
watch

I Am Sick

Purpose: To introduce talking about illness

Teacher Preparation and Materials

Pictures of people with obvious illness or pains

Warm-up

1. Show pictures of people who are obviously ill or in pain (or act out different symptoms or pains). Ask *What is wrong? What is happening?* Elicit or provide words such as *sick, hurt,* or *pain.* If learners provide names of any body parts, write them on the board.

2. Show pictures again. Ask *What do you think this person will say? What do you think the person will do?* Encourage learners to provide words such as *doctor, call,* or *telephone.*

Presentation

1. Have learners turn to page 45 and look at the person in the picture. Ask *What is wrong? What is happening?*

2. Direct learners' attention to the title at the top of the page and say *I am sick.* Have learners repeat. Make sure learners understand the meaning of *sick.* Encourage them to act out the meaning or give examples.

3. Ask learners to act out symptoms they often have when they are sick. Model by first saying *I am sick.* Then act out a symptom, such as coughing. Write the word *cough* on the board, say it, and have learners repeat. Ask learners to demonstrate other symptoms. Write the words on the board.

Expansion/Extension

• Draw a simple outline of a body (or just a stick figure with hands and feet) on the board. Say *I have a pain,* and act out feeling pain in a body part, such as an arm or the back. Point to that area of the body on the board and draw jagged lines or arrows to indicate pain. Say the name of the body part, and write it on the board next to it. Have learners repeat. Ask learners to point to other places on their bodies where they often have pain. Elicit or provide the

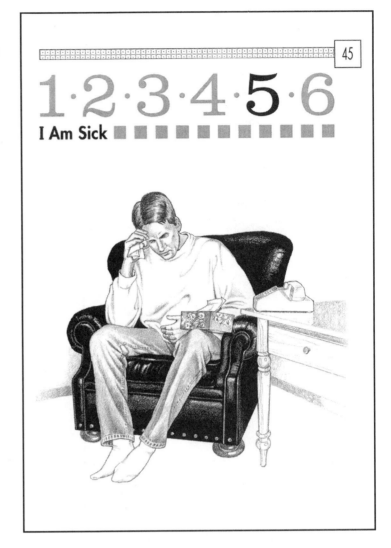

words for the body parts and write them on the board, connecting each word to the appropriate part of the body on the board.

• Use the picture on page 45 and other pictures of sick people to model, and have learners use third person pronouns and forms of the verb *be.* Point to a picture, say *He is sick,* and have learners repeat. Follow a similar pattern to elicit *She is sick* and *They are sick.*

Calling the Doctor

Purpose: To introduce calling a doctor's office for an appointment; to give practice in describing symptoms

Teacher Preparation and Materials

1. Pictures of a doctor, doctor's office, sick people
2. ▩▩▩ Audiotape for Literacy Level
3. Two real or toy telephones *(Expansion/Extension)*

Warm-up

Show pictures of sick people. For each, ask *What's wrong? What's happening? What will the person do?* Prompt learners to suggest that the person will go to or call a doctor. Hold up a picture of a doctor. Ask *Who is this?* Elicit or give the word *doctor,* write the word on the board, and have learners repeat. Show a picture of a doctor's office. Ask *Where is this?* Elicit or give the word *office,* write it on the board, and have learners repeat.

Presentation

1. Have learners turn to page 46 and look at the pictures. Point to picture one and ask Where? Elicit or say *doctor's office,* write it on the board, say the phrase again, and have learners repeat. Have learners label the picture of the doctor's office. Point to the second picture and ask *Where?* Depending on learners' responses, write *home, house,* or *apartment* on the board and say it. Have learners repeat and label the picture.

2. Have learners label the last two pictures themselves. Ask learners who is talking and what they think the people are talking about.

3. ▩▩▩ Play the audiotape of the story, and have learners listen with their books closed. ▩▩▩ Play the audiotape again, and have them follow along in their books. Read the story aloud, and have learners read along with you.

4. Ask learners to look at the first picture and chorally read the sentence under it. Ask what words they already know, and elicit what those words mean. Have learners act them out or point to things in the

picture. Help them identify words they do not know and clarify meaning. Have learners read the sentence again. Repeat the process for each of the pictures and captions. When finished, ask learners if their earlier guesses about what the characters are saying were right.

Expansion/Extension

Using toy or real telephones, have a volunteer act out the conversation with you. Pair learners, and have them practice the conversation. Then, have each pair come to the front and use the telephones to act out the conversation in front of the class, if possible without using their books as reference.

The Body

Purpose: To introduce and give practice in identifying body parts

Teacher Preparation and Materials

1. Audiotape for Literacy Level
2. Pictures of various types of people showing full bodies (*Expansion/Extension*)

Warm-up

1. Draw a stick figure on the board. Invite volunteers to come up and point to and name parts of the body for which they know the words. Write the words they say. Draw a line from each word to the body part, say the word, and have all learners repeat.

2. Play the audiotape. As learners listen, have them point, on their own bodies, to the parts of the body that they recognize.

Presentation

1. Have learners turn to page 47 and look at the picture of the body. Play the audiotape again, and have learners follow along with the list of words on the page. Have them look at the body part connected to each numbered line as the numbered items are said on the tape.

2. Point to the first word and say *Number 1, eye, eye.* Have learners repeat. Ask *Where is the eye?* and indicate that you want learners to point to it. When they do, point to the eye to confirm and then point to the line connected to the eye. Have learners copy the word onto the blank line next to the number 1. Repeat this process for each body part.

3. Play Simon Says with parts of the body. Have learners stand in a circle and say either *Simon says touch your . . .* or *Touch your . . .* If someone touches a body part when *Simon says* is not said, the person sits down.

4. Have learners remain in a circle. Starting at the eye, each learner names the next body part encountered as one moves down the body. Name only the body parts taught in the lesson. Repeat, but start at the feet and move toward the eye.

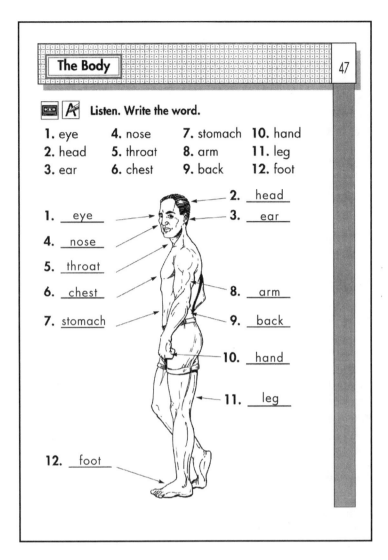

The Body 47

Listen. Write the word.

1. eye	4. nose	7. stomach	10. hand
2. head	5. throat	8. arm	11. leg
3. ear	6. chest	9. back	12. foot

1. _eye_
2. _head_
3. _ear_
4. _nose_
5. _throat_
6. _chest_
7. _stomach_
8. _arm_
9. _back_
10. _hand_
11. _leg_
12. _foot_

Expansion/Extension

- Divide the class into teams of three or four learners. Say *I am thinking of a body part that starts with* f. The first team that guesses *foot* gets a point. Continue with *n, t, c, h* (two), *a, b, l, e* (two), and *s.* For the letters that have two body parts, follow the first *I am thinking . . .* with *I am thinking of another body part that starts with . . .*

- Give learners pictures of people showing the full body. Ask them to label the parts of the body. Have learners identify other parts of the body that they want to know. Say those words, and spell them for the learners. Then have them label those parts on their pictures.

Parts of the Body

Purpose: To give practice in identifying body parts; to give practice in recognizing words with rhyming sounds

Teacher Preparation and Materials

1. Large drawing of a stick figure or whole body on chart paper
2. ▦ Audiotape for Literacy Level
3. Blank paper, one sheet for each learner *(Expansion/Extension)*

Warm-up

Post the drawing of the stick figure or whole body in the front of the room. Have learners call out the name of a body part. Point to a body part on the drawing that either matches or does not match what the learners called out. Have them say if it is right or wrong. If wrong, have them point to the correct body part on themselves. Continue until all parts listed on page 47 are named at least once.

Presentation

1. Have learners individually complete the first exercise on page 48. Ask them to compare answers with the person sitting next to them.

2. Put a series of three words on the board: *leg, beg, peg.* Point to the first word, and ask learners if they know it. Ask learners to say it. Repeat the word. Point to the other two words, and ask learners if they recognize them. They will probably say no. Point to the *b* in *beg.* Ask the learners to name the letter. Ask them to give the sound that the letter makes. (If they do not respond, write several *b* words that they know to remind them. [FOR EXAMPLE: *board, book, back*]) Write *leg,* and ask them to pronounce it again. Erase the *l* and replace it with *b.* Ask them to combine the *b* sound and the *eg* with you. Pronounce *beg* several times. Repeat with *peg.* Practice with several other sets of rhyming words. FOR EXAMPLE: *nose, pose, rose; chest, test, nest; pen, hen, men; name, game, fame.*

3. ▦ Play the audiotape, and have learners complete the second exercise. To check answers, write the initial word for each item

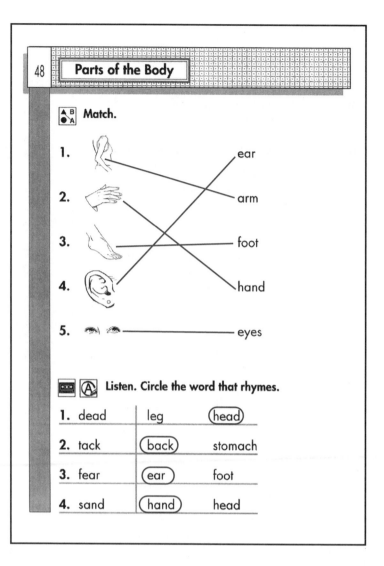

on the board and say it. Ask a volunteer to say the rhyming word and spell it. Write it on the board next to the initial word. Then say the pair with the learners chorally.

Expansion/Extension

Have learners write *The Body* at the top of a sheet of paper and put numbers 1–12 down the side. Go through the list of body parts from page 47. For each one, ask *How many? One? Two?* Have learners write the number and the word, in appropriate singular or plural form, for each part. Give learners any irregular plural forms, such as *feet.*

What's Wrong?

Purpose: To give practice in describing symptoms and health problems

Teacher Preparation and Materials

Cards or pieces of paper with health problems written on them (FOR EXAMPLE: *My leg hurts. I have a fever.*) *(Expansion/Extension)*

Warm-up

Pantomime being sick. First indicate pain in some part of your body. Ask *Where?* Have learners name the body part. Ask for a volunteer to write the word for the body part on the board. (Others in the class can spell the word for the learner, if necessary.) Repeat the process several times with different body parts. Then say *I am sick.* Cough, and ask learners *What?* Elicit or provide the word *cough.* Write the word on the board. Repeat the process to elicit or teach *runny nose* and *fever.*

Presentation

1. Write the sentence *My . . . hurts.* Pantomime the first pain from the *Warm-up.* Have learners call out the body part again. Point to the word. Say *What's wrong? My . . . hurts* (insert the name of the body part from the board). Have learners repeat. Pantomime the next pain, ask *What's wrong?* and signal learners to answer. Repeat with all body parts in the unit that are appropriate for this structure.

2. Have learners turn to page 49, look at the picture in item 1 in the exercise, and read the example sentence. Have them complete items 2 and 3. Check answers by asking *What's wrong?* and having volunteers say the answer.

3. Write the sentence *I have a . . .* Pantomime the first symptom, *fever.* Have learners say the word. Point to it on the board. Say *What's wrong? I have a fever.* Have learners repeat. Say *What's wrong?* and signal learners to answer. Repeat with *cough* and *runny nose.*

4. Have learners read the example in item 4 and complete items 5 and 6. Check answers by asking *What's wrong?* and having volunteers say the answer.

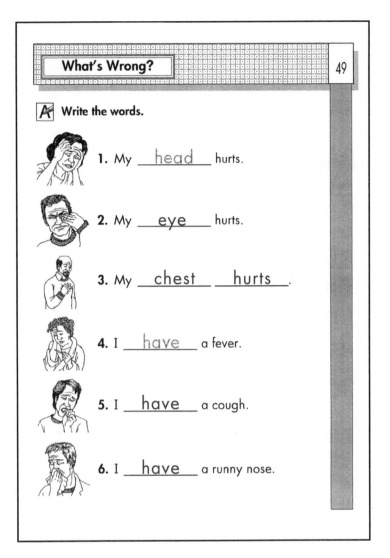

Expansion/Extension

- Have a pile of cards or pieces of paper with ailments written on them (FOR EXAMPLE: *My leg hurts. I have a fever.*) Have a learner come forward and draw a card. The learner acts out the ailment. The other learners ask, "What's wrong?" The first learner states the problem from the card. Repeat until all learners have a chance.

- Point to a body part or symptom listed on the board. Have half the class ask "What's wrong?" and the other half respond with the appropriate sentence ("I have a . . ." or "My . . . hurts"). Do the same with pairs of individual learners.

Can You Come at 3:00?

Purpose: To give practice in calling a doctor's office with a health problem; to introduce expressing time

Teacher Preparation and Materials

1. Cards with numbers 1–12 (or number cards from Handout 6)
2. A real or toy analog clock with movable hands, with hours numbered
3. ▓▓▓ Audiotape for Literacy Level

Warm-up

1. Have learners turn to page 46 and review the conversation. ▓▓▓ Play the audiotape for page 46. Divide the class in half. Have half the learners read the receptionist's lines and the other half read the patient's lines. Ask learners to guess what the characters might say next.
2. Review numbers 1–12 by holding up cards and having learners call out the number.
3. Introduce expressing times. Show learners the hours numbered on a real or toy analog clock. Point to each number and have learners say it. Put the hands of the clock at 1:00, say *one o'clock,* and have learners repeat. Write 1:00 on the board, say it, and have learners repeat. Do the same for the other hours.

Presentation

1. ▓▓▓ Have learners turn to page 50 and follow the conversation as they listen to the audiotape. Have them identify the parts of the dialogue that are the same as the one they practiced on page 46. Have them pantomime the ailments that the patient reports. Then have them identify what is different about this dialogue. Read the last exchange between the receptionist and the patient, and have learners repeat. Ask *What time?* and elicit "At 3:00."
2. Have learners look at the picture at the bottom of the page. Ask *What is happening in the picture? Where are the people now?* Ask *What time?* Have learners point to the clock in the picture and give the time.

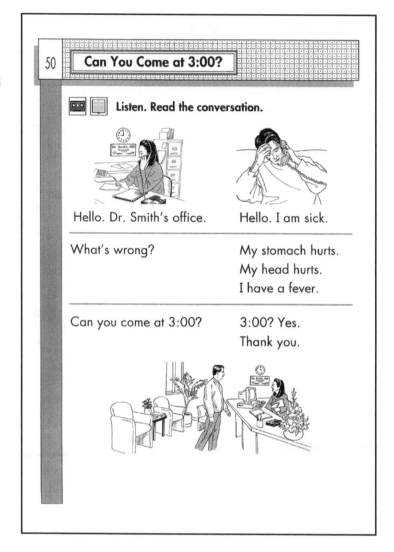

3. Divide the class in half again, and practice the complete conversation. Have one half read the receptionist's lines and the other half read the patient's lines.
4. Put the learners in pairs, and have the pairs practice the conversation, with each partner taking a turn saying each role.

Expansion/Extension

- Have pairs of learners say the conversation again, but insert different times. Prompt by moving the hands of the clock to different hours.
- Give learners alternate phrases to use in the conversation. FOR EXAMPLE: Replace *I am sick* with *I don't feel well.* Provide other ailments, such as *My arm hurts, I have a sore throat,* or *I have pain in my chest.*

At 3:00?

Purpose: To give practice in telling time and saying the hours

Teacher Preparation and Materials

1. A watch, an analog clock (with movable hands), and a digital clock, or pictures of each

2. Copies of Handout 17, Telling Time (one clock for each learner, with the hands attached and movable, using paper clips)

3. Pictures of people doing activities typical of certain times of the day (sleeping, waking up, eating lunch, working, etc.) *(Expansion/Extension)*

Warm-up

Show learners a watch, an analog clock, and a digital clock, or pictures of each. Ask *What is this?* for each item. Elicit or give the words *watch* and *clock*. Write the words on the board, and say them. Have learners repeat. Point to the clock in the room, and ask *What is it?* Point to your watch or a learner's watch, and ask *What is it?* Ask all learners wearing watches to raise their hands.

Presentation

1. Have learners turn to page 51, and look at the pictures at the top of the page. Point to each, and ask what it is. Elicit *watch, clock,* and *clock.* Have learners label the pictures.

2. Ask learners what is written under each picture. Point to each and say *Three o'clock* or *It's three o'clock.* Ask learners, *What time is it?* Point to the times, and say *It's three o'clock.* Have learners repeat.

3. Give each learner a copy of the clock from Handout 17. Point to the hours going around the clock, and say *hours.* Have learners repeat. Point to the numbers for the hours, and have learners call them out.

4. Move the hands on the analog clock to read one o'clock. Have learners do the same on their clocks. Say *one o'clock.* Have learners repeat. Repeat the process for all the hours.

5. Put learners in pairs. Ask one learner to model the activity with you. Move the hands on your clock to three o'clock, and

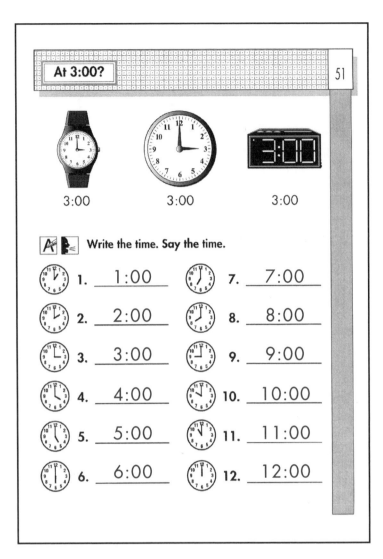

say *three o'clock,* but do not show the clock. Have the learner move the hands on his clock to illustrate the time. Have the learner show you his clock and ask you "3:00?" Show your clock, and say *Yes, three o'clock.* Have pairs practice, using various times.

6. Draw a clock face on the board showing one o'clock. Ask learners *What time is it?* Write 1:00 next to the clock. Direct learners to do the same on line one of the exercise. Have learners write the times for the other clock faces.

Expansion/Extension

Introduce the concepts of A.M. and P.M. using pictures of activities typical of certain times of the day (sleeping, waking up, eating lunch, working, going to school, etc.).

What Time Is It?

Purpose: To give practice in telling time

Teacher Preparation and Materials

1. Clocks with movable hands from Handout 17, Telling Time (one clock for each learner)

2. An analog clock with movable hands (or an enlarged version of the clock from Handout 17)

Warm-up

Show various times using an analog clock with movable hands. Use only hours, and ask *What time is it?* Have learners call out the times. Then move the hands to show 3:10 and ask *What time is it?* If no one responds, say *It's three ten.*

Presentation

1. Draw a large clock face on the board similar to the one on page 52, with the hours numbered and the minutes marked and numbered up to 15. Have learners turn to page 52 and look at the picture at the top. Point to the hours, and ask what they are. Write *hours* on the board with an arrow pointing to a number. Say *hours;* have learners repeat and copy the word in their books. Point to the minutes. Say *minutes,* and write the word on the board with an arrow pointing to the minutes. Have learners repeat and copy the word in their books.

2. Have learners start at 1 and move around the clock, counting off the minutes. (Learners may need some help with 50 and 60, as they have not practiced those numbers, but they will know the pattern.)

3. Have learners look at the clocks in the middle of the page. Ask *What time is it?* Elicit the response "three ten." Point to the 3 and say *hours;* point to the 10 and say *minutes.* Write various other times on the board, and have learners say them. Prompt by pointing to the individual numbers in the time, if necessary.

4. Give each learner one of the clocks with movable hands. Move the hands on your clock to read 3:15, and have learners do the same. Point to the hour hand at 3, and say *three hours.* Point to the minute hand

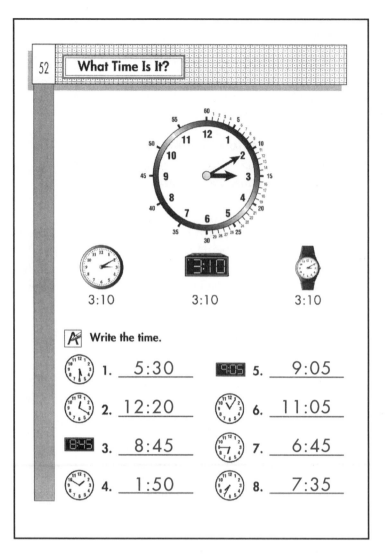

3:10   3:10   3:10

Write the time.

1. 5:30   5. 9:05

2. 12:20   6. 11:05

3. 8:45   7. 6:45

4. 1:50   8. 7:35

at the 3, and say *fifteen minutes.* Say *three fifteen.* Have learners repeat. Repeat the process with additional times.

5. Have learners write the times shown on the clock faces in the exercise at the bottom of the Student Book page. Have them compare answers with the person next to them.

Expansion/Extension

- Say a time, and have learners illustrate it on their clocks. Have learners compare with your clock or with the clock of the person next to them.

- Introduce other terms for time increments on the clock, such as *quarter past, half past, quarter to.*

Time

Purpose: To give practice in listening to and identifying times and numbers

Teacher Preparation and Materials

1. Copies of Handout 18, Number Bingo (cut into cards, enough so that each learner has at least one card)
2. Coins, beans, or similar small objects that learners can use to mark their bingo cards
3. ▦ Audiotape for Literacy Level

Warm-up

Have learners play Number Bingo to practice listening for numbers. If necessary, demonstrate how to play the game and how to mark the bingo cards.

Presentation

1. Ask learners what time it is. Repeat the number back as a question to confirm the time. Write the time on the board. Ask what time class starts and what time it finishes. Write those times on the board. Ask learners what time they do various activities during the day (work, eat lunch, sleep, study, watch TV, and so on). Have several learners respond for each activity.

2. Say a series of times (hours alone and hours plus minutes). Have learners write down the times. Check answers as a class.

3. Have learners turn to page 53. ▦ Play the audiotape, and have learners complete the first exercise. Have them compare answers with the person next to them.

4. ▦ Play the audiotape, and have learners complete the second exercise. Check answers. Give additional practice with any pairs that learners found confusing.

Expansion/Extension

- Say activities from a daily schedule. FOR EXAMPLE: *At 6:30 I get up. I eat breakfast at 7:15. I go to work at 8:30.* and so on. Have learners write the times that they hear.

- Make additional copies of the bingo cards from Handout 17, but change the numbers to times. Play Time Bingo.

- Ask learners to make a list of the numbers they think are difficult to say or to understand in speech. Give practice in

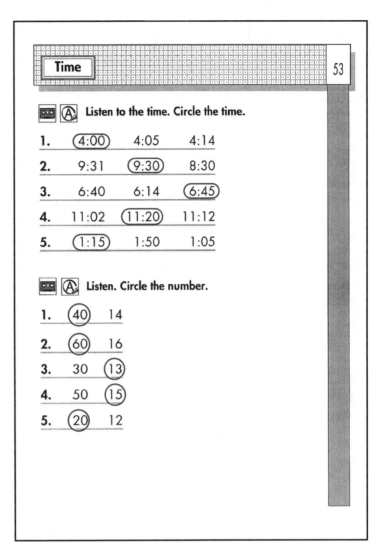

saying those numbers and in listening to and distinguishing them.

- Have learners draw or bring in pictures from magazines showing activities they do during a normal day (FOR EXAMPLE: get up, eat, work, study, play with children, watch TV). Have them put the pictures in the order in which they do the activities, then write the time they do each activity on or next to its picture. Learners can describe their daily schedules to the class.

Dr. Smith's Office

Purpose: To give practice in calling a doctor's office, expressing a health problem, and getting an appointment

Teacher Preparation and Materials

1.  Audiotape for Literacy Level
2. Copies of Handout 19, I Am Sick Story (one copy for each learner and one for each pair of learners) *(Expansion/Extension)*

Warm-up

Say *I am sick.* Pantomime various pains or symptoms. Have learners identify the ailments as you act them out. Ask learners *What can I do?* Elicit responses such as "Call the doctor" or "Go to the doctor."

Presentation

1. Have learners turn to page 54 and look at the pictures at the top of the page. Ask *Who are these people? Where are they? What is wrong with the person in the second picture?* Have learners brainstorm various symptoms and write them on the board.

2.  Play the audiotape for page 50, giving the conversation between the receptionist and the patient. Have learners listen first with their books closed.  Play the tape again, and have them listen again with their books open, following the conversation on the page.  Play the tape a third time, stopping between sentences if necessary, and have learners write the missing words on the lines.

3. Review the conversation as a class. Have individual learners say a sentence and spell the word that goes in the blank. When the conversation is complete, have pairs of learners say the whole conversation.

Expansion/Extension

- Give each learner a copy of Handout 19. Have learners draw speech bubbles on the pictures and copy the conversation from page 54 into the appropriate speech bubbles.

- Have learners work in pairs. Give each pair a clean copy of Handout 19. Have them create their own conversation, using alternate phrases and different symptoms.

They can also choose a different time for the appointment and change the clock in the picture. They can again draw speech bubbles on the picture and write the conversation in the bubbles. Have pairs present their conversation to the class.

123456 Summary
I Want a Job

Objectives

Functions
- Identifying and naming jobs
- Giving personal information on an application

Life Tasks
- Identifying ways to find a job
- Looking for a job
- Reading job ads
- Completing a job application
- Identifying job hours and salaries

Structures
- Simple present tense verbs
- *I am a . . .*

Culture
- Looking for a job in the United States

Vocabulary

Key words:

application
city
construction worker
friend
help wanted sign
housecleaner
job
job experience
look for
mechanic
newspaper
read
salesperson
state
talk
waiter
want
work
zip code

Related words:
classifieds
fill out
full-time
interview
part-time
pay
paycheck
salary

I Want a Job

Purpose: To introduce vocabulary for common workplaces

Teacher Preparation and Materials

1. Pictures of places where learners might have jobs, FOR EXAMPLE: a restaurant dining room or kitchen, a department or grocery store, a gas station or car repair shop, a school, a hotel (lobby or guest room), a construction site

2. A copy of Handout 12, Neighborhood Places, enlarged if possible, using only the cards showing the places

3. A picture of someone clearly outside, preferably working outside, and a picture of someone clearly inside, again preferably working *(Expansion/Extension)*

Warm-up

1. Review names of places in a neighborhood. Show pictures from Handout 12, and have learners name each place. Write the words on the board.

2. Write the words for common workplaces on the board (FOR EXAMPLE: *restaurant, store, school, gas station, hotel*). Show pictures to clarify meaning. Say the name of the place, and have learners repeat.

Presentation

1. Have learners turn to page 55 and look at the pictures of workers. Ask *Who are these people? What are they doing?* Write any words that the learners produce on the board.

2. Point to one of the pictures of a worker on page 55, and ask learners where they would find this person. If necessary, show a picture used in the *Warm-up* to prompt learners, or let a volunteer come up and find an appropriate picture. Repeat until the workplace for each worker is named.

Expansion/Extension

- Have learners rank their preferences for the jobs shown. Model by expressing your own preference. Point to the worker with the job you like best (perhaps the teacher) and say, for example, *I like this. This is best* or *This is number one.* Use facial expressions and tone of voice to express preference. Elicit the same information from learners. Then elicit the job each learner thinks is the worst. If possible, have them indicate the order for jobs that fall in between the two.

- Introduce the concept of inside jobs and outside jobs. Number each worker pictured on page 55 and have learners do the same. On the board, tape a picture of someone obviously outside and write *outside* below it. Tape a picture of someone obviously inside and write *inside* under it. Have learners categorize the jobs on page 55 as inside or outside jobs. Put the number of the job under the correct category. Ask learners which they prefer, inside or outside work.

Robert Wants a Job

Purpose: To introduce ways to look for a job

Teacher Preparation and Materials

1. ▣▣ Audiotape for Literacy Level
2. A picture or model of a sports car (or other luxury item)

Warm-up

Act as if you are thinking, and say *I want a pencil* (or other object easily seen in the room). Repeat. Walk around and look for someone who has a pencil. Stop at that person's desk and repeat *I want a pencil*. Say this until the person gives you the pencil. Act as if you are thinking again, and say *I want a book*. Repeat until someone gives you a book. Do this with two other objects easily found in the room. Finally, hold up the picture or model of a sports car, and say *I want a sports car*. Show it to a learner or two, and ask *Do you want a sports car?* If possible, elicit a yes answer, and prompt the learners to also say "I want a sports car."

Presentation

1. Have learners turn to page 56. Point to the picture of Robert and say *This is Robert Chang*. Have learners repeat. Ask *What is his first name? What is his last name?* and have learners indicate his first and last names. Say *Robert Chang wants a job*. Point to the other pictures. Ask *What is Robert doing?* Record on the board any words that learners produce.

2. ▣▣ Play the audiotape. Have learners listen and follow the story while looking only at the pictures. Have them point to each picture as the caption is said.

3. Review the meaning of new words to check comprehension. Act out or, if possible, have learners act out the verbs *talk, read,* and *look for.*

4. Have the learners look at the words below the pictures. Have them find the new words in the story and circle them. ▣▣ Play the audiotape again, asking learners to listen for those words. When the tape is finished, have learners say the words at the bottom of the page. Check, and if necessary, review pronunciation.

56 Robert Wants a Job

▣▣ ▣ Listen. Read the story.

My name is Robert Chang.

I want a job.

I read the newspaper.

I talk to friends.

I look for help wanted signs.

Have learners draw an arrow from each circled word to the object in the picture that it represents.

5. Have the class read the story aloud chorally. Then have individuals read the story aloud. Encourage them to act out the verbs as they read.

Expansion/Extension

Learners can say the story but make it about themselves. They can use their own names and say only the things that they do (or did) to find a job. Provide words if they want to mention other things they do to find a job. (FOR EXAMPLE: I talk to family members. I look at bulletin boards.)

I Want a Job

Purpose: To give practice with vocabulary for finding a job; to introduce two forms of regular present tense verbs

Teacher Preparation and Materials

Pictures of people engaged in common activities (FOR EXAMPLE: working, reading, writing, shopping, eating)

Warm-up

Have learners review the story on page 56. Have them read it aloud as a class. Ask questions about the story, pointing to the picture for each question: *Who is talking? What does he want? What does he read? Who does he talk to? What does he look for?*

Presentation

1. Have learners turn to page 57 and look at the exercise at the top of the page. Read the first sentence, *Robert wants a ___.* Ask learners *What? What does Robert want?* Have them call out the answer, and then write it in the blank. Repeat for each of the sentences. To check answers, write the words on the board, or ask volunteers to copy the complete sentences on the board.

2. Write *job, newspaper, friends,* and *help wanted signs* on the board in a column. Write *wants, reads, talks,* and *looks* in another column. Label the first column *Things.* Label the second column *Actions.* Discuss the differences between the two lists. Have learners give the words for additional things and actions that they know.

3. Have learners look at the first item in the second exercise. Ask them what is different and what is the same in the two sentences. Point out that the form of the action word changes depending on the person doing the action. Have learners complete the exercise.

4. Read the sentence pairs in the second exercise. Have learners repeat. Focus on having them hear and pronounce the final *-s.* At this point, however, they will not consistently produce the third person *-s* in speech.

I Want a Job

A Write the words.

1. Robert wants a _____job_____.
2. Robert reads the ___newspaper___.
3. Robert talks to ___friends___.
4. Robert looks for ___help wanted___ signs.

A Underline what is different.

1. <u>I want</u> a job.   <u>Robert wants</u> a job.

2. <u>I read</u> the newspaper.   <u>Robert reads</u> the newspaper.

3. <u>I talk</u> to friends.   <u>Robert talks</u> to friends.

4. <u>I look</u> for signs.   <u>Robert looks</u> for signs.

---

5. Show pictures of people doing common activities. As much as possible, use verbs that have been used in previous lessons (FOR EXAMPLE: *read, write, shop, work*). Elicit the words, and write them on the board. Have learners write sentences beginning with *I* and with *Robert,* using the correct form of the verb

Expansion/Extension

- Go over the sentences in the book and the ones learners have written, substituting the names of other characters in the Student Book (FOR EXAMPLE: *Susan* or *Alex*).

- Introduce the pronoun *he* as a substitute for *Robert.* Have learners write and say sentences replacing *Robert* with *he.* Write or review sentences containing *Susan;* introduce the pronoun *she.* Have learners write and say the sentences using *she.*

You Want a Job

Purpose: To give practice with final -s on verbs; to give practice in giving simple yes and no responses to questions with *do*

Teacher Preparation and Materials

▆▆▆ Audiotape for Literacy Level

Warm-up

Put a list of five or six singular and plural word pairs (nouns or verbs from previous lessons) on the board. Point to the first pair, and say either the singular or plural form. Ask the learners *Do you hear* s*?* Repeat the question, pointing first to the form with the -s and then to the form without it. Repeat the word and the question. Ask learners to indicate yes or no. Repeat the word, and underline the one you are saying to show learners if they heard correctly. Repeat for each of the pairs.

Presentation

1. Have learners turn to page 58 and look at the first exercise. Explain that they will listen for the same sound as they did in the *Warm-up.* ▆▆▆ Have learners listen to the audiotape and complete the exercise. Do the first one together as an example if necessary. Circulate to check answers. Call on individuals to say the words they circled in each item. If learners have trouble hearing or saying any of the items with final -s, give additional practice.

2. Write a chart on the board like the one in the second exercise, with the three sentences and a space for a check. Say *Robert Chang wants a job. What does he do?* Point to the first sentence. Ask *Does Robert read the newspaper?* Have learners respond yes or no. Check the sentence to indicate yes. Repeat the process for the next two questions.

3. Have learners look at the second exercise. Ask *What do you do? Do you read the newspaper?* Read each question and have learners put a check mark by the things that they do to find a job. Call on learners to say the things that they do.

4. Have learners practice asking the questions with "Do you . . . ?" to elicit the sentences in the exercise. Have them repeat

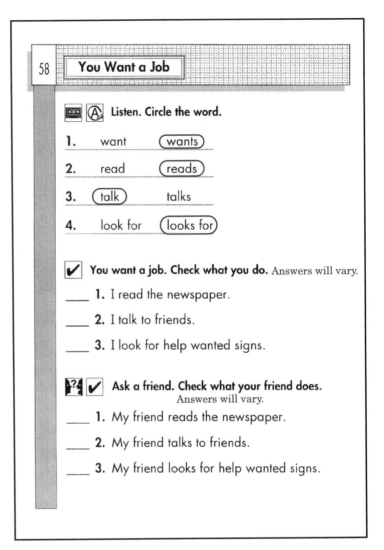

the questions several times until they are comfortable asking them. Then put them in pairs and have them ask about and record what their partner does to find a job.

Expansion/Extension

Ask learners questions with *Do you . . . ?* using other verbs that the class has learned. FOR EXAMPLE: *Do you shop on Tuesday? Do you work outdoors?* Have learners respond. With learners, brainstorm a set of questions using this pattern. Write the questions on the board, and have learners practice asking them. Then put learners in pairs, and have them ask and respond to each other.

I Talk to My Friends

Purpose: To give practice with vocabulary for jobs

Teacher Preparation and Materials

1. ▦ Audiotape for Literacy Level

2. Cards or slips of paper with the name of one of the jobs presented in this lesson written on each (one set for every three learners) *(Expansion/Extension)*

3. Pictures of people in the jobs taught in the unit: teacher, waiter, cook, construction worker, auto mechanic, salesperson

Warm-up

1. Show pictures of people in jobs. Have learners look at the pictures and name the jobs that they know. Write on the board any words that they produce. Say the words. Have learners repeat.

2. Have learners turn to page 55 and look again at the people pictured there. Have them name jobs that they know.

Presentation

1. Have learners look at the first sentence and the picture at the top. Ask *Who is talking? What is he saying?* Tell learners that Robert is talking to his friends about their jobs. ▦ Play the audiotape, and have the learners listen and follow along. Have them point to each picture at the bottom of the page as the corresponding sentence is read. When the tape is finished, point to each job and say the word for the job. Have learners repeat.

2. Ask learners *Do you have any friends who have these jobs? Do you know anyone with one of the jobs?* Point to the first picture and say *Do you have a friend who is a teacher?* Have learners say yes or no and if yes, to raise their hands. All learners should be able to give your name as a teacher they know. Have learners write the names of their friends next to the appropriate picture. Repeat for each picture. (If no learners know someone with a particular job, show a picture of someone with that job and make up a name for the person. (FOR EXAMPLE: *This is Alfredo. He is a mechanic.*)

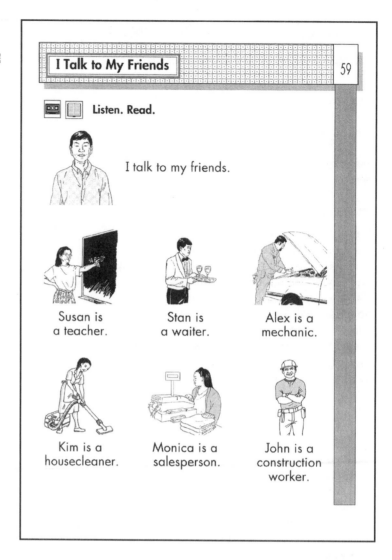

▦ ▨ Listen. Read.

I talk to my friends.

Susan is a teacher.

Stan is a waiter.

Alex is a mechanic.

Kim is a housecleaner.

Monica is a salesperson.

John is a construction worker.

3. As a class, read the sentences under the pictures again. Pair learners. Have them substitute the names of their friends in the sentences and say the new sentences to their partner.

Expansion/Extension

- Have the names of the jobs written on cards or slips of paper. Put learners in groups of three and give each group a set of the cards. Each learner draws a slip of paper and acts out a job. The others must guess the job. When each learner in a group has had a turn, have each draw a second slip and repeat.

- Have learners draw, act out, describe, or name jobs that other friends have but that were not covered in this lesson. Write the jobs on the board and have learners copy and say them.

Jobs

Purpose: To give practice with vocabulary for jobs; to allow learners to identify their own jobs

Teacher Preparation and Materials

1. Pictures of people in various jobs (the ones used on page 59 and others, showing a mix of men and women)

2. Materials to make bulletin board displays or posters (FOR EXAMPLE: chart paper or poster board, blank paper for each learner, markers, scissors, glue or tape, magazines with pictures that can be cut out) *(Expansion/Extension)*

Warm-up

Hold up one picture of a man doing a job and another of a woman doing a job. Have learners identify the jobs. Model the sentences *He is a . . .* and *She is a . . .* Have learners repeat. Hold up various pictures, and have learners identify them using the model sentences.

Presentation

1. Have learners turn to page 60 and complete the matching activity. Check answers by pointing to each picture and having volunteers identify the job by saying "He is a . . ." or "She is a . . ."

2. Ask learners to identify their own jobs. Model, saying *I am a teacher*. With a learner whose job you know, model *I am a . . .* Have that learner repeat. If learners know their job name, have them say the sentence. If not, have them draw a picture of the job, the job setting, or the job tools. As a class try to figure out what the job is. Write the names of the jobs on the board so that learners can copy their job (and the others). Have each learner write his or her job on the line in the Student Book. If any learners are not working, suggest alternatives. (FOR EXAMPLE: I am a student; I am a homemaker; I am retired.) On separate paper, have all learners draw a picture representing their job. If they prefer, they can bring in an appropriate picture.

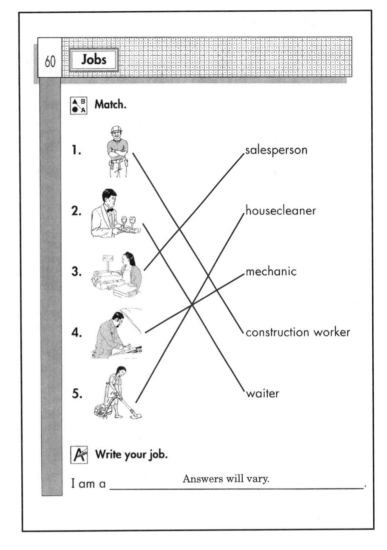

Expansion/Extension

- Have learners create bulletin board displays or posters about work that can be hung in the room. Divide the class into groups to brainstorm words that they have learned dealing with work and to create a written presentation of them; to make or cut out pictures from magazines, showing jobs, job tools, and job settings. Have each learner fill a piece of paper with this sentence: "_____ (learner's name) is a _____ (learner's job)" and any pictures or decorations desired. Have each learner add this to the bulletin board or a poster.

- Ask learners to name the job or jobs that they had in their native countries; introduce the sentence *I was a . . .* Ask what they want to be in the future; introduce *I will be a . . .*

I Read the Newspaper

Purpose: To give practice in reading a simple job ad

Teacher Preparation and Materials

1. Cards with days of the week, several times (9:00, 7:00, 3:00, 5:00, etc.), and dollar amounts written on them
2. A newspaper with a classified section of job ads
3. Copies of Handout 21, Finding a Job in the Newspaper (one copy for each learner) *(Expansion/Extension)*

Warm-up

1. Ask learners what information they want about a job. Write on the board the words the learners say. Prompt if necessary with cards showing days of the week, times, and dollar amounts.
2. Ask learners who are currently working what days and hours they work. Create a chart or grid on the board with columns for name, job, days, and hours.

Presentation

1. Have learners turn to page 61 and look at the picture in the top left. Ask learners to identify Robert Chang. Remind them that Robert reads the newspaper to help him find a job.
2. Have learners look at the job ad on page 61. Ask *What is it?* Elicit or give the word *ad.* Have learners repeat. Ask *What do you think the ad is about?* Put on the board any ideas they suggest. Use a newspaper to show learners where to find job ads.
3. Have the learners look again at the ad. Ask if they recognize anything in the print. Have them read aloud any information they can. Then read the whole ad. Read the ad again, line by line, and have learners repeat. Ask *What information is the ad giving?* Go over each item. Ask *What is a salesperson? What is Monday to Friday? What is 1:00–5:00? What is $9.00/hour?* Teach *salary* or *pay.* Model how to say the salary listing in the ad (nine dollars an hour).

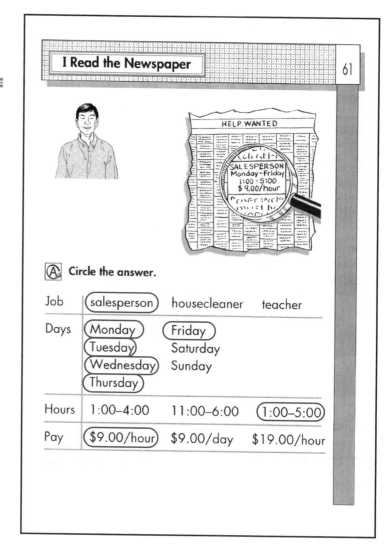

4. Have learners use the information in the ad to circle the correct answers in the exercise at the bottom of the page.
5. Have learners discuss and write their preferences or availability for the categories from the ad (job, hours, days, pay). Ask if this would be a good job for them. Discuss.

Expansion/Extension

Give learners copies of Handout 21, Finding a Job in the Newspaper. Have learners read the job ads and discuss the information in each. Ask questions to check comprehension. Have them complete the comparison chart on the handout. Then have learners compare the jobs with the preferences they wrote earlier. Discuss whether any of the jobs are good ones for them.

A Job Application

Purpose: To introduce filling out job applications

Teacher Preparation and Materials

1. Copies of Handout 20, The United States (one per learner)
2. Picture of a salesperson and a waiter
3.  Audiotape for Literacy Level
4. Copies of simple job applications from local businesses
5. Large copy of the application on page 62, on chart paper or the board

Warm-up

1. Review personal information. Ask learners *What is your last name? Your first name? Where do you live? What is your address? What is your telephone number?* Have learners respond orally.
2. Show samples of simple job applications. Ask *What is this?* Elicit or say *application*. Have learners repeat.

Presentation

1. Have learners look at the picture on page 62. Ask *Who are the people? Where are they? What do you think they are saying?*
2. Play the audiotape, and have learners follow the words in the speech bubbles. Ask learners to point to the application on the page. Ask them to guess what *fill out* means. Demonstrate if necessary. Check comprehension. Ask *What does Robert want?* (a job) *What does he do?* (fill out an application)
3. Have learners look at the large copy of the application. Have volunteers come forward to circle and say one word that they recognize. Continue until there are no more volunteers.
4. Write the words from the application that the learners recognized (*name, first, last, address, telephone,* etc.). Say each one, and have learners say the word or information that Robert filled in for it.
5. List on the board words learners didn't recognize (possibly *city, state, zip, job experience*). Explain the words, and give examples to clarify. Name the city in which

your school is located. Have learners name the cities where they live. Name the state in which the school is located. Use Handout 20 to show other states. For job experience, use Robert Chang as the example. Say, *Now he is looking for a job. But in the past he was a salesperson and a waiter.* Show pictures, and have learners identify the jobs. Have learners name their current jobs (I am a . . .) and then ask them to name jobs they had in the past (I was a . . .).

Expansion/Extension

Call out parts of the job application or key words (*name, zip,* etc.), and have learners circle, underline, or check the parts named. Have learners make a list of the types of information asked for on applications.

Your Job Application

Purpose: To give practice in filling out a job application

Teacher Preparation and Materials

1. Large map of the United States
2. Large map of the state in which your school is located
3. Handout 20, The United States (one for each learner)
4. Handout 22, Job Application (one for each learner) *(Expansion/Extension)*
5. Blank paper for each learner

Warm-up

1. Have learners turn to page 62 and look at Robert Chang's job application. Randomly call out words for information requested on the form and have learners say Robert's information (FOR EXAMPLE: *name:* Robert Chang, *telephone number:* (713) 881-3650)

2. Randomly call out words for information requested on an application, and have individuals answer about themselves.

Presentation

1. Have learners turn to page 63 and read the information about Robert at the top of the page. If necessary, review *first name* and *last name* once more.

2. Have learners look at the first picture on the next line. Ask *What is it?* Elicit *United States;* then point to the dot on the map and ask again to elicit *city.* Ask *What city does Robert live in?* (Houston) Have learners look at the next picture. Repeat to elicit *state* and *Texas.* With the next picture, point to the *address* and have them say *address.* Review the meaning of *zip.* Ask learners to say Robert's zip code. Ask them to count and say how many numbers are in a zip code. (5)

3. Show a large map of the United States. Help learners find their state on it. Give each learner a copy of Handout 20. Have learners circle their state. Then show a large map of the state, and help learners find their city. Have them put a dot for their city on their maps. Have them write their zip code at the bottom.

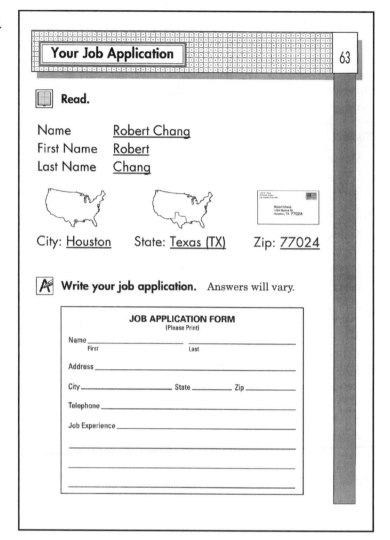

4. Ask learners to look at the job application at the bottom of the page. Have them write each category of information requested, one per line on a sheet of paper. Have learners individually write their information on the correct line of the paper. Have each learner exchange their papers with the person next to them. That person goes over it and, if there are any questions, discusses or clarifies with the writer. When everything seems correct, learners copy their information onto the application.

Expansion/Extension

Have learners copy their information to fill out the job application on Handout 22. Tell learners they can take that with them to copy when they need to fill out a real application.

I Am a Salesperson

Purpose: To give practice in writing and talking about one's job

Teacher Preparation and Materials

1. ▓▓ Audiotape for Literacy Level
2. Large copy of the story frame from page 64, on chart paper or on the board
3. Blank paper *(Expansion/Extension)*

Warm-up

Have learners turn to page 56 and look at the second picture of Robert. Point to the thought bubble. Ask *What job does Robert want? What does Robert want to be?* (a salesperson) Let learners discuss whether they think Robert gets the job.

Presentation

1. Have learners turn to page 64 and look at the picture at the top of the page. Ask *Who is it?* (Robert) *What is he doing? Did he find a job? What is Robert's job?* (salesperson)

2. ▓▓ Play the audiotape, and have learners follow in their books. ▓▓ Play the audiotape again if necessary. Have learners read the story aloud, chorally and then individually.

3. Check comprehension. Ask *Who is talking? What is Robert's job? When does he work? What days? What hours?*

4. Have learners write the type of information Robert is giving in each line of the story: name, job, days, hours. Write these categories on the board. After each one, write the information about you. Read the information, and have learners read along with you.

5. Use a copy of the story frame to rewrite the story with your information in place of Robert's. Have learners tell you what to write on each line. Read the new story together as a class.

6. Have learners write their own story, filling in information about themselves in the story frame at the bottom of the page. If learners are not working, help them write alternative information. (FOR EXAMPLE: I am a student. I study on . . . I am a volunteer at . . . I am a mother/father.)

7. Put learners in groups of three or four, and have them read their stories to each other. In a small class, have them read the stories to the whole class.

Expansion/Extension

Learners can copy their personal stories onto clean paper. If they wish to add any information, help with new words. They can illustrate the stories or bring in pictures from magazines to paste onto their paper. Post these stories around the room for all learners to read and discuss. If possible, duplicate the stories to create a class book.

Tapescripts

UNIT 1
Welcome to English Class

page 6   Welcome
Narrator: Listen to the conversation.
Susan: Welcome to English class.
Alex: Thank you.
Susan: My name is Susan.
Alex: My name is Alex.

Page 8   The Alphabet
Narrator: Listen to the letters. Say the letters. Trace and write the letters.

A
B
C
D
E
F
G
H
I
J
K
L
M
N
O
P
Q
R
S
T
U
V
W
X
Y
Z

Page 10   Letters and Sounds
Narrator: Listen. Circle the word you hear.
1. name
2. Susan
3. English
4. class
5. welcome

UNIT 2
Personal Information

Page 15
Narrator: Listen to the conversation.
Susan: Hello, Alex.
Alex: Hello, Susan.

Page 16   Names and Introductions
Narrator: Listen to Alex's story.
Alex: Hello.
            My name is Alex Marcos.
            My first name is Alex.
            My last name is Marcos.
            I am from Mexico.

Page 17   Personal Information
Narrator: Listen to Susan's story.
Susan: My name is Susan Davis.
            My first name is Susan.
            My last name is Davis.
            I am from the United States.
            I am married.
            I have two children.

Page 19   Practicing Numbers 0 to 5
Narrator: Listen. Circle the number you hear.
1. zero
2. five
3. two
4. one

Page 23 Words and Sounds

Narrator: Listen. Circle the letter that begins the words you hear.

1. married, mother, Marcos
2. sister, son, single
3. David, daughter, Don
4. family, father, five

UNIT 3
In the Neighborhood

Page 26 Alex Lives Here

Narrator: Alex lives at 5243 Walnut Street.

Page 32 Telephone Numbers

Narrator: Listen to the telephone number. Circle yes or no.

1. 398-2746
2. 332-5169
3. 947-4318

Page 33 My Telephone Number

Narrator: Listen to the stories.

Alex: My name is Alex Marcos.
            My telephone number is 713-691-8836.

Susan: My name is Susan Davis.
            My telephone number is 713-886-5192.

UNIT 4
Going Shopping

Page 36 Going Shopping: When?

Narrator: Listen to Monica's story.
Monica: I shop on Saturday.
Narrator: When?
Monica: Saturday.

Page 37 Days of the Week

Narrator: Listen to Monica's story.
Monica: I work on Tuesday and Thursday.
            I go to school on Monday and Wednesday.

Page 39 Going Shopping: Where?

Narrator: Listen to Monica's story.
Monica: I shop at the supermarket.
Narrator: Where?
Monica: The supermarket.

Page 41 How Much?

Narrator: Listen to the conversation.
Customer: How much?
Clerk: $3.20, please.

Page 43 Paying for Food

Narrator: Listen. Circle the price you hear.

1. Chicken is $3 a pound.
2. That will be $8.12.
3. Your total is $12.25.
4. Fourteen dollars, please.
5. Thirty-nine cents.

Page 44 I Shop on Friday

Narrator: Listen to the conversation.
Customer: I shop on Friday.
            I shop at the supermarket.
            I shop for chicken, bread, and milk.
Clerk: $24.19, please.

UNIT 5
I Am Sick

Page 46 Calling the Doctor

Narrator: Listen to the conversation.
Receptionist: Hello. Dr. Smith's office.
Jim: Hello. I am sick.
Receptionist: What's wrong?
Jim: My stomach hurts. My head hurts. I have a fever.

Page 47 The Body

Narrator: Listen. Write the word you hear.

1. eye
2. head
3. ear
4. nose

5. throat

6. chest

7. stomach

8. arm

9. back

10. hand

11. leg

12. foot

Page 48 Parts of the Body

Narrator: Listen. Circle the word that rhymes.

1. dead

2. tack

3. fear

4. sand

Page 50 Can You Come at 3:00?

Narrator: Listen to the conversation.

Receptionist: Hello. Dr. Smith's office.

Jim: Hello. I am sick.

Receptionist: What's wrong?

Jim: My stomach hurts. My head hurts. I have a fever.

Receptionist: Can you come at 3:00?

Jim: 3:00? Yes. Thank you.

Page 53 Time

Narrator: Listen to the time. Circle the time you hear.

1. At 4:00

2. Can you come at 9:30?

3. Can you come at 6:45?

4. At 11:20.

5. Can you come at 1:15?

◆ ◆ ◆

Narrator: Listen. Circle the number you hear.

1. 40

2. 60

3. 13

4. 15

5. 20

UNIT 6
I Want a Job

Page 56 Robert Wants a Job

Narrator: Listen to Robert's story.

Robert: My name is Robert Chang.

I want a job.

I talk to friends.

I read the newspaper.

I look for help wanted signs.

Page 58 You Want a Job

Narrator: Listen. Circle the word you hear.

1. wants

2. reads

3. talk

4. looks for

Page 59 I Talk to My Friends

Narrator: Listen to Robert's story.

Robert: I talk to my friends.

Susan is a teacher.

Kim is a housecleaner.

Stan is a waiter.

Monica is a salesperson.

Alex is a mechanic.

John is a construction worker.

Page 62 A Job Application

Narrator: Listen to the conversation.

Robert: I want a job.

Receptionist: OK. Fill out this job application.

Page 64 I Am a Salesperson

Narrator: Listen to Robert's story.

Robert: My name is Robert Chang

I am a salesperson.

I work on Monday, Tuesday, Wednesday, Thursday, and Friday.

I work from one o'clock to five o'clock.

◆ ◆ ◆

Photocopy Masters

Resource Activities and Self-Assessment Tools

1 **Drawing Shapes**
To recognize and practice drawing common shapes;
to practice hand-eye coordination . . . . Use before Unit 1

2 **Recognizing Shapes**
To recognize similarities and differences of shapes . . . . Use before Unit 1

3 **Following Directions**
To become familiar with exercise directions and symbols
representing directions used in the Student Book. . . . . Use before Unit 1

4 **Strip Story**
To practice reading simple sentences; to sequence a simple story. . . . . Use with Unit 1

5 **Student Interview Chart**
To practice greeting others and introducing self;
to practice spelling and writing names . . . . Use with Unit 1

6 **Number Cards**
To practice recognizing and saying numbers . . . . Use with Units 2, 3, 4

7 **My Family**
To identify and write the names of family members . . . . Use with Unit 2

8 **Checking In—Units 1 and 2**
To self-assess individual progress in Units 1 and 2 . . . . Use after Units 1 and 2

9 **Letter Cards (Capitals)**
To practice recognizing, saying, and writing the alphabet
in capital letters . . . . Use with Unit 1

10 **Letter Cards (Lowercase)**
To practice recognizing, saying, and writing the alphabet
in lowercase letters. . . . . Use with Unit 3

Using the Resource Activities and Self-Assessment Tools

| **Handouts** |

The handouts in this section provide teachers with ready-made materials and resources to complement, reinforce, or expand the lessons in the Literacy Level Student Book. The handouts include materials to provide additional practice, to reinforce learners' emerging literacy skills, or to challenge more advanced learners.

In general, the handouts are referenced within specific lesson notes in the Teacher's Edition. Some, such as Strip Story, Neighborhood Signs, Money, Telling Time, and Neighborhood Places, are used in activities that provide practice or reinforcement within the unit lessons. Others, such as Student Interview Chart, My Family, and My Calendar, involve students in activities that ask them to apply language presented in the Student Book lessons to real life. A few handouts, such as the map of the United States, are intended primarily as general resources as well as the basis for lesson expansion activities.

The handouts are designed to be flexible. While the list of handouts on pages 99–100 indicates a unit for which each one is suitable, many of the activities could be used at various points in the Student Book to expand or review concepts in the lessons. Teachers can also use the handouts as the basis for creating additional activities or as models for their own activities. For example, a teacher could photocopy the food cards on Handout 15, cut them out, and paste them over the numbers on the Number Bingo handout to create a vocabulary bingo. The Strip Story (Handout 4) and its suggested activities can be a model for creating strip stories from other readings or conversations in the Student Book.

| **Checking In: Self-Assessment Tools** |

Assessment, and particularly self-assessment, is an important element of the learning process and should be an integral part of any instruction. However, at the literacy level, formal tests may be unfamiliar and even intimidating to learners. To introduce learners to assessment in a non-threatening and level-appropriate fashion, three pages called "Checking In," one for every two units in the Student Book, are provided in this section for use as self-assessment tools. These pages list the principal concepts presented in the units, with spaces for learners to record what they feel they know or do not know after completing the units.

| **General Procedure for Using Checking In** |

1. Photocopy Checking In, one copy for each learner.
2. Ask students to brainstorm what they have talked about, written, and learned in the two units covered by Checking In. Write or draw their responses on the board.
3. Pass out the sheets. Have learners, as a group, match their brainstorm responses to the items listed on the sheet. If the learners have identified any items not already listed, add them at the bottom. Draw attention to items on the list that learners did not mention.
4. As a group, discuss the first item on the list. Have learners open the Student Book and elicit or direct them to the specific pages on which the item was presented to help them remember the context in which it was taught and to be sure that all learners understand what the term refers to. If the item is a category or grouping of vocabulary words or a set of numbers or letters, show how only a few examples are listed on

the sheet, and make sure learners understand the use of ellipsis points (. . .) to show there are other items in the category. Ask learners for more examples.

5. Show students the direction icons for *Write, Read, Say,* and *Listen,* and ask them to think about whether they can use the items on the list in those language modes. Then ask the learners to decide individually if they feel they know or don't know the item, and have them mark the appropriate column on their page. The first Checking In asks learners simply to respond to a smiling or frowning face, to indicate how they feel about their ability with an item. On the second and third Checking In, the faces are associated with print *(I know; I don't know).*

6. After learners have completed their self-assessments, ask them to circle the items they feel they need—or want—to practice more. Review the pages and discuss them with individual learners to decide how to address items that need more individual practice, or have the group as a whole decide what items they all need to review.

Checking In is not a test; it does not ask learners to produce language learned in the units. It simply provides prompts that learners can use to reflect on and recognize their progress.

Drawing Shapes

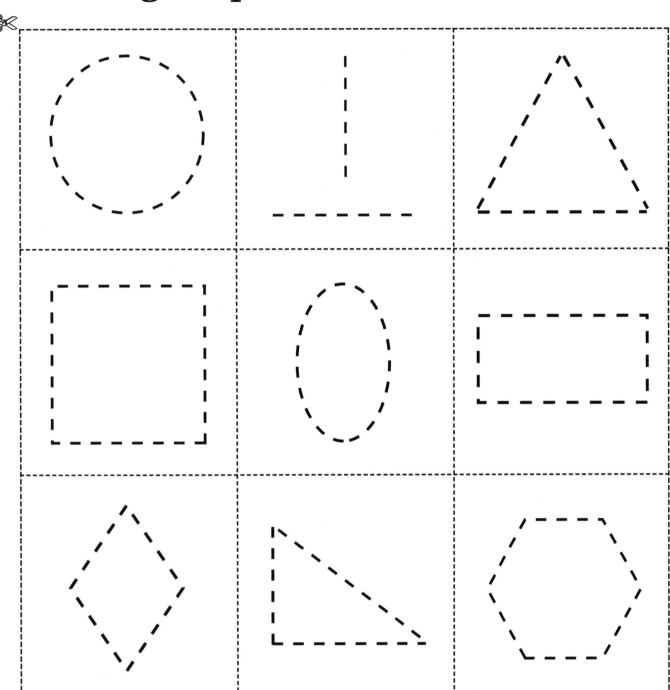

Recognizing Shapes

Ⓐ CIRCLE THE SAME SHAPE.

1.	○	□	□	○	□
2.	△	◇	◇	◇	△
3.	◡	◡	○	○	○
4.	◇	▽	◇	▽	▽
5.	□	▭	▭	□	▭
6.	⬡	□	⬡	□	□

Ⓐ CIRCLE THE DIFFERENT SHAPE.

1.	L	L	L	⌐	L
2.	⊕	⊕	⊘	⊕	⊕
3.	↑	↑	↑	↑	↓
4.	V	Λ	V	V	V
5.	S	S	S	Ƨ	S
6.	O	C	O	O	O

Following Directions

WRITE

UNDERLINE

READ

LISTEN

SAY

MATCH

CIRCLE

CHECK

DRAW

TRACE

LOOK

ASK

Strip Story

 WELCOME TO ENGLISH CLASS.

 THANK YOU.

 MY NAME IS SUSAN.

 MY NAME IS ALEX.

Student Interview Chart

HELLO.

MY NAME IS _____.

1.	
2.	
3.	
4.	
5.	
6.	
7.	
8.	

Number Cards

0	5	1_	6_
1	6	2_	7_
2	7	3_	8_
3	8	4_	9_
4	9	5_	1_

My Family

 DRAW YOUR FAMILY.

WRITE THE NAMES.

MY FAMILY

MY NAME _____

FATHER _____

MOTHER _____

BROTHERS _____

SISTERS _____

HUSBAND/WIFE _____

CHILDREN _____

Checking In—Units 1 and 2

✔ CHECK WHAT YOU KNOW.

MY NAME IS _____.		
A, B, C, D, E, F, . . . Y, Z		
BOOK DESK . . .		
HELLO		
FIRST NAME		
LAST NAME		
I AM FROM _____.		
0, 1, 2, 3, 4, 5		
FAMILY, BROTHER, MOTHER, CHILDREN . . .		
SINGLE, MARRIED		

Letter Cards (Capitals)

A	G	N	U
B	H	O	V
C	I	P	W
D	J	Q	X
E	K	R	Y
F	L	S	Z
	M	T	

Letter Cards (Lowercase)

a	g	n	u
b	h	o	v
c	i	p	w
d	j	q	x
e	k	r	y
f	l	s	z
	m	t	

Neighborhood Signs

☑ **Check the signs in your neighborhood.**

	Yes	No
1. STOP		
2. DO NOT ENTER		
3.		
4.		
5. H		
6.		

Neighborhood Places

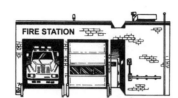
police station

fire station

supermarket

bank

post office

drugstore

hospital

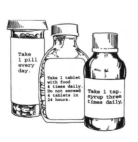

My Calendar

Sunday					

Money

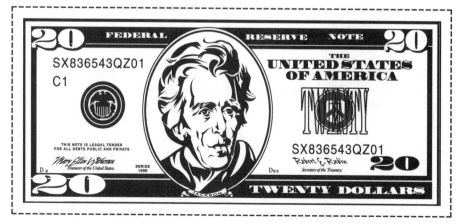

Food

chicken	fish	beef	pork
carrots	potato	corn	tomato
bread	rice	pasta	flour
milk	eggs	cheese	butter
grapes	banana	orange	apple

Checking In—Units 3 and 4

 Check what you know.

	I know	I don't know
Addresses: 5243 Walnut Street		
a, b, c, d, e, f, . . . y, z		
Signs: STOP DO NOT ENTER		
post office, school, bank . . .		
Numbers: 0–49		
Telephone numbers: (307) 398-2746		
911		
Monday, Tuesday, . . . Saturday, Sunday		
When? Where?		
carrot, milk, eggs, chicken . . .		
Money:		

Telling Time

Number Bingo

44	39	51
26	60	8
1	15	17
6	23	59

4	25	9
0	11	23
35	52	41
18	5	60

21	14	60
35	0	62
46	19	3
7	55	12

13	24	6
50	29	53
12	15	32
2	47	10

HANDOUT 18

I Am Sick Story

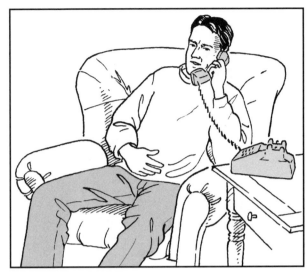

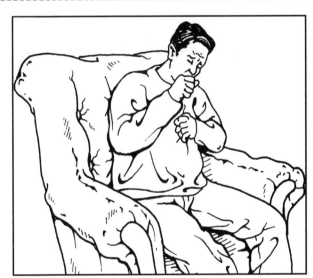

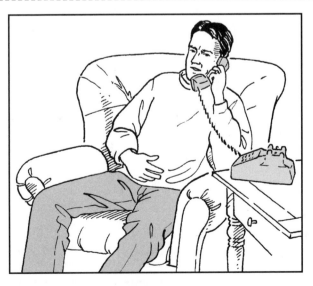

The United States

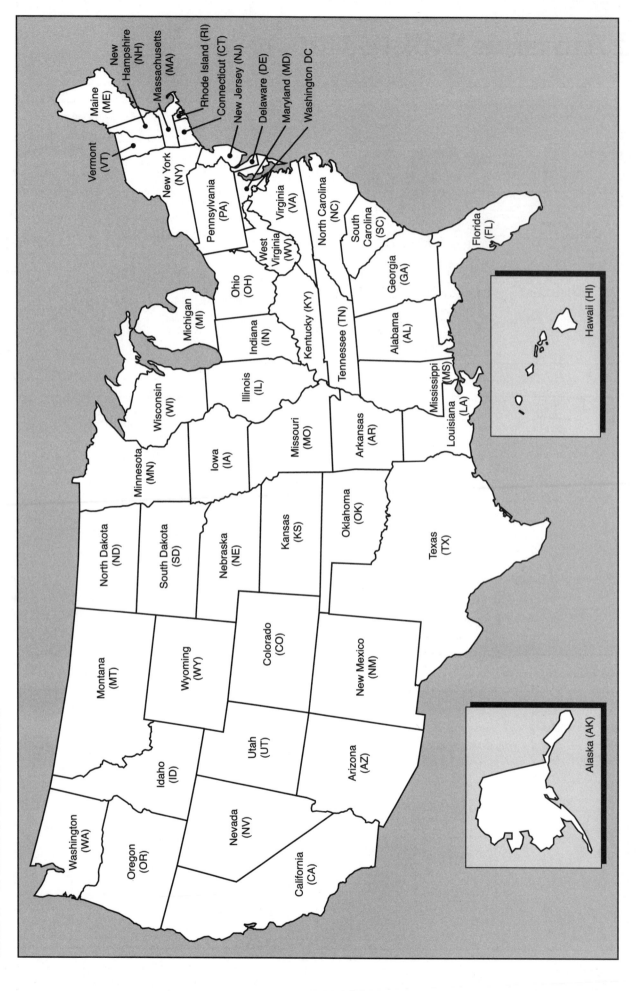

Finding a Job in the Newspaper

WAITER
Friday - Sunday
4:30-11:00
$8.00/hour

HOUSE CLEANER
Tuesday - Sunday
9:00-5:00
$9.50/hour

CONSTRUCTION WORKER
Monday - Thursday
7:00-2:00
$14.50/hour

SALES CLERK
Monday - Friday
8:00-4:00

JOB	DAYS	HOURS	PAY

Job Application

JOB APPLICATION FORM
(Please Print)

Name _____ _____
         First   Last

Address _____

City _____ State _____ Zip _____

Telephone _____

Job Experience _____

_____

_____

_____

_____

_____

_____

_____

_____

Checking In—Units 5 and 6

✔ **Check what you know.**

	I know	I don't know
arm, throat, eye, back . . .		
I am sick.		
My _____ hurts.		
I have a _____ .		
Time:		
want, read, talk, look for		
I read. Robert reads.		
Jobs: teacher, salesperson, mechanic . . .		
Monday–Friday 1:00–5:00		
city, state, zip		
job application		

Index of Functions

Index of Structures